BE A PEOPLE PERSON

This book is an opportunity to see in distilled form what John Maxwell has been learning and using successfully throughout a productive life. Be a People Person *is a book of help. Even the table of contents stimulated my thinking and made me ask questions about myself which is, after all, the first prerequisite for personal growth. The questions I asked, he answered.*

Fred Smith

BE A PEOPLE PERSON

John C. Maxwell

Chariot Victor Publishing
A Division of Cook Communications

Chariot Victor Publishing, a division of
Cook Communications, Colorado Springs, Colorado 80918
Cook Communications, Paris, Ontario
Kingsway Communications, Eastbourne, England

Recommended Dewey Decimal Classification: 301.155
Suggested Subject Heading: LEADERSHIP

ISBN: 1-56476-264-5

22 23 24 25 26 27 28 29 30 31 Printing/Year 04 03 02 01

CONTENTS

This book is dedicated to the three con-gregations that I have been privileged to pastor.

*The Church of Christ
in Christian Union
Hillham, Indiana
1969-1972*

*Faith Memorial Church
Lancaster, Ohio
1972-1980*

*Skyline Wesleyan Church
Lemon Grove, California
1981-*

These churches represent thousands of relationships that have molded me as a leader. It is from these experiences that this book has been written. The one truth that rings clearer than any other is . . .

People don't care how much you know until they know how much you care.

FOREWORD

If God ever created a perfect people person, it is John Maxwell. By his mere entrance into a room he draws people to attention, excites them to enthusiastic response, and motivates them to action. His genuine charisma exudes warmth and a caring spirit, and in this day of electronic preachers and glitzy leaders, John Maxwell stands as a rock of integrity. In the years I have known John as a friend and fellow speaker, I have observed that what you see is what you get. There is no guile or duplicity in his life, and what path he directs others to take he has already walked himself.

One of my great personal joys is having the opportunity to work with John in leadership seminars and enjoy the electricity he generates in an audience. Although John has exceptional platform skills, it is his behind-the-scenes sincerity that impresses me the most. He chooses staff members who have strength in their areas of expertise and he helps make them stronger. He encourages their individuality and is secure enough in his own heart that he doesn't need yes men to make him look good. He has one of the few successful ministries with men, and his discipleship program combines challenge with accountability.

You will enjoy John's sense of humor and his ability to

tell stories with excitement and emotion. You will be motivated to look at difficult people in a more understanding way, and if you put John's principles into practice, you will never be the same again.

Florence Littauer
San Bernardino, California

1.

WHAT DRAWS ME TO PEOPLE?

Understanding the qualities you enjoy in others

The basis of life is people and how they relate to each other. Our success, fulfillment, and happiness depends upon our ability to relate effectively. The best way to become a person that others are drawn to is to develop qualities that we are attracted to in others.

Just as I was preparing for this chapter, I received an anonymous card from a member of my congregation. It was especially meaningful because it reflected the importance of warm, rewarding relationships:

> When special people touch our lives then suddenly we see how beautiful and wonderful our world can really be. They show us that our special hopes and dreams can take us far by helping us look inward and believe in who we are. They bless us with their love and joy through everything they give. When special people touch our lives they teach us how to live.

Does that reflect the kind of person you are to others? It was a humbling blessing for me to receive such a greeting card. I realized how appropriate it is to this chapter as we consider what qualities we need to develop in our lives

—the qualities we enjoy in others.

This poster in a Nordstrom department store once caught my attention: "The only difference between stores is the way they treat their customers." That's a bold statement. Most stores would advertise the quality of their merchandise or their wide selection as what sets them apart from the rest. The difference between Nordstrom and other stores, according to an employee of the competition, is that other stores are organization-oriented; Nordstrom is people-oriented. Their employees are trained to respond quickly and kindly to customer complaints. As a result, according to writer Nancy Austin, "Nordstrom doesn't have customers; it has fans."

A study by TARP, Technical Assistance Research Programs, in Washington, D.C., shows that most customers won't complain to management if something goes wrong with the purchase. But TARP found out that, depending on the severity of the problem, an average customer will tell between 9 and 16 friends and acquaintances about his bad experience. Some 13 percent will tell more than 20 people! More than two out of three customers who've received poor service will never buy from that store again and, worse, management will never know why.

Every company is bound to goof now and then, but from the customer's perspective, what's important is that the company responds. This is the secret of the Nordstrom success. The TARP study also shows that 95 percent of dissatisfied customers will buy from the store again if their problems are solved *quickly.* Even better, they will each tell eight people of the situation's happy conclusion. The trick for managers and salespeople is to give customers ample time to offer feedback on the service they receive.

This chapter certainly isn't about department stores and customer satisfaction, but there are some principles from these reports that should speak to us about our relationships with others:

☐ Are we quick to respond to others' needs?

☐ Do we run from problems or face them?

☐ Do we talk more about bad news or good news?
☐ Do we give people the benefit of the doubt or do we assume the worst?

The Golden Rule

What's the key to relating to others? It's putting yourself in someone else's place instead of putting them in their place. Christ gave the perfect rule for establishing quality human relationships. We call it the Golden Rule, a name it got sometime around the seventeenth century. Near the end of the Sermon on the Mount, Christ summed up a series of profound thoughts on human conduct by saying, "Therefore whatever you want others to do for you, do so for them" (Matt. 7:12).

In this brief command, Christ taught us a couple of things about developing relationships with others. We need to decide how we want to be treated. Then we need to begin treating others in that manner.

Recently I took my daughter Elizabeth out to a restaurant for lunch. The waitress whose job it was to take care of people, made us feel that we were really inconveniencing her. She was grumpy, negative, and unhelpful. All of her customers were aware of the fact that she was having a bad day. Elizabeth looked up at me and said, "Dad, she's a grump, isn't she?" I could only agree with her. Everything we asked of the waitress was met with a look of disdain.

Halfway through our experience I tried to change this lady's negative attitude. Pulling out a $10 bill I said, "Could you do me a favor? I'd like some change for this $10 bill, because I want to give you a good tip today." She looked at me, did a double take, and then ran to the cash register. After changing the money, she spent the next fifteen minutes hovering over us. I thanked her for her service, told her how important and helpful she was, and left a good tip.

As we left, Elizabeth said, "Daddy, did you see how that lady changed?"

Seizing this golden opportunity I said, "Elizabeth, if you want people to act right toward you, you act right toward them And many times you'll change them."

Elizabeth will never forget that lesson because she had seen a noticeable change take place right before her eyes. That grumpy lady didn't deserve to be treated kindly. But when she was treated not as she was, but as I wanted her to be and believed she could become, her perspective suddenly changed.

Whatever your position in a relationship, if you are aware of a problem, it's your responsibility to make a concerted effort to create a positive change. Quit pointing your finger and making excuses, and try being a catalyst by demonstrating and initiating the appropriate behavior. Determine not to be a *reactor* but an *initiator*.

Five Ways You Want Others to Treat You

These next five points seem too simple to even mention, but somehow we overlook them. The qualities that make relationships right aren't complicated at all. There's not a person reading this who doesn't need, like, or respond to these qualities in others.

First, you want others to encourage you. There is no better exercise for strengthening the heart than reaching down and lifting people up. Think about it; most of your best friends are those who encourage you. You don't have many strong relationships with people who put you down. You avoid these people and seek out those who believe in you and lift you up.

Several years ago Dr. Maxwell Maltz' book, *Psychocybernetics,* was one of the most popular books on the market. Dr. Maltz was a plastic surgeon who often took disfigured faces and made them more attractive. He observed that in every case, the patient's self-image rose with his or her physical improvement. In addition to being a successful surgeon, Dr. Maltz was a great psychologist who understood human nature.

A wealthy woman was greatly concerned about her son,

and she came to Dr. Maltz for advice. She had hoped that the son would assume the family business following her husband's death, but when the son came of age he refused to assume that responsibility and chose to enter an entirely different field. She thought Dr. Maltz could help convince the boy that he was making a grave error. The doctor agreed to see him, and he probed into the reasons for the young man's decision.

The son explained, "I would have loved to take over the family business, but you don't understand the relationship I had with my father. He was a driven man who came up the hard way. His objective was to teach me self-reliance, but he made a drastic mistake. He tried to teach me that principle in a negative way. He thought the best way to teach me self-reliance was to never encourage or praise me. He wanted me to be tough and independent. Every day we played catch in the yard. The object was for me to catch the ball ten straight times. I would catch that ball eight or nine times, but always on that tenth throw he would do everything possible to make me miss it. He would throw it on the ground or over my head but always so I had no chance of catching it."

The young man paused for a moment and then said, "He never let me catch the tenth ball—never! And I guess that's why I have to get away from his business; I want to catch that tenth ball!"

This man grew up feeling he could never measure up, never be perfect enough to please his father. I would not want to be guilty of causing emotional damage to my wife, my children, or my friends by not giving them every opportunity to succeed.

When Elizabeth and I used to play Wiffleball, I would pitch and she would swing. I told her it was my responsibility to hit the bat with the ball. Once she had swung at least twenty times without making contact with the ball. Finally in desperation and disgust she said, "I need another pitcher; you can't hit the bat!" I was duly brought low for my failure to let her succeed. I have since done better.

The story of Eugene Lang gives us an ultimate example of encouragement. Entrepreneur Lang was *Success* magazine's "Successful Man of the Year" in 1986. The following is part of a feature article about Lang's encouragement of others.

A gray-haired man stands alone in the center of the auditorium stage—a distinguished, paternal presence sporting a fine wool suit and the barest trace of a mustache. He scans the sunlit room, with its peeling paint and frayed draperies, but his gaze lingers on the people.

They are black and Hispanic men and women who fill most of the seats in the auditorium. Though some do not speak English, their attention is fixed on the man at the podium. But his speech is not aimed at them. He has returned to this place where he once was a student to address the 61 sixth graders, dressed in blue caps and gowns, who are seated in the front rows.

"This is your first graduation—just the perfect time to dream," he says. "Dream of what you want to be, the kind of life you wish to build. And believe in that dream. Be prepared to work for it. Always remember, each dream is important because it is *your* dream, it is your future. And it is worth working for."

"You must study," he continues. "You must learn. You must attend junior high school, high school, and then college. You can go to college. You must go to college. Stay in school and I'll . . ." The speaker pauses, and then, as if suddenly inspired, he blurts out: "I will give each of you a college scholarship."

For a second there is silence, and then a wave of emotion rolls over the crowd. All the people in the auditorium are on their feet, jumping and running, cheering and waving and hugging one another. Parents rush down the aisles to their children. "What did he say?" one mother calls out in Spanish. "It's money! Money for college!" her daughter yells back with delight, collapsing into her parent's arms.

The place was an elementary school in a poverty-stricken, drug-ridden, despair-plagued Harlem neighborhood. The speaker was multimillionaire entrepreneur Eugene Lang, who 53 years earlier had graduated from that very school. The date was June 25, 1981, and the big question was whether the warm and ever-confident Lang, a man who believes that "each individual soul is of infinite worth and infinite dignity," would fulfill his promise.

Well, he did and he still is. In fact, these kids are now getting ready to graduate from high school and only one has dropped out of high school since the sixth grade. You have to understand, in this community, 90 percent of the kids drop out of high school.

Lang began the "I Have a Dream" foundation and now other entrepreneurs in New York City are also going into classrooms offering the same kind of scholarships. Now there are 500-600 kids in Harlem who will receive this reward if they don't drop out of school.

People need to be encouraged. Eugene Lang believed in these kids and it made all the difference in how they lived the rest of their lives.

Lang's students speak confidently of becoming architects, computer experts, entrepreneurs of all types. Lang says 25 will go to college this year; the others will have high school diplomas, opportunities for vocational training and, eventually, jobs. "This approach is exactly right," observes Charles Murray of the Manhattan Institute of Policy Research, whose book *Losing Ground* laments that poor people are losing their drive to climb the ladder of success.

Ari Alvarado expressed it from the students' side: "I have something waiting for me," he said, "and that's a golden feeling." And if this program works, it may in fact become the ultimate capitalist success story—for, as George Gilder points out, the roots of capitalism lie not in greed but in giving: The true capitalist is one who invests money and energy today in hopes of a return in the uncertain future. That's what Eugene Lang has done, and it's likely that some of his dream students will follow suit. "I want to become a doctor and do well so I can adopt a class of my own someday," says the optimistic Alvarado. "Just think, if all of us adopted classes . . . it could spread across the world!"

That is exactly what Eugene Lang hopes will happen: "We have to create the opportunity to work with hope, to work with ambition, and to work with self-respect. The rewards? There is no way to describe the joy of having a young person touch your arm and smile because you have taught him new values and touched his heart and mind. The greatest experience you can have is to see that child with his new aspirations.

The happiest people are those who have invested their time in others. The unhappiest people are those who wonder how the world is going to make them happy. Karl Menninger, the great psychiatrist, was asked what a lonely, unhappy person should do. He said, "Lock the door behind you, go across the street, find someone who is hurting, and help them." Forget about yourself to help others.

You Want Others to Appreciate You

William James said, "The deepest principle in human nature is the craving to be appreciated."

Have you heard the story about the young politician's first campaign speech? He was very eager to make an impression on his audience, but when he arrived at the auditorium, he found only one man sitting there. He waited, hoping more people would show up, but none did. Finally he said to the one man in the audience, "Look, I'm just a young politician starting out. Do you think I ought to deliver this speech or dismiss the meeting?"

The man thought a moment and replied, "Sir, I'm just a cowhand. All I know is cows. Of course, I do know that if I took a load of hay down to the pasture and only one cow came up, I'd feed it!"

Principle: We cannot underestimate the value of a single person.

With the advice from the cowhand, the politician began his speech and talked on and on for two hours as the cowhand sat expressionless. Finally he stopped and asked the cowhand if the speech was all right.

The man said, "Sir, I am just a cowhand and all I know is cows. Of course, I do know that if I took a load of hay down to the pasture and only one cow came up, I surely wouldn't dump the whole load on him."

Principle: Don't take advantage of people.

J.C. Staehle, after analyzing many surveys, found that the principle causes of unrest among workers were the following, listed in order of their importance:

1. Failure to give credit for suggestions.
2. Failure to correct grievances.
3. Failure to encourage.
4. Criticizing employees in front of other people.
5. Failure to ask employees their opinions.
6. Failure to inform employees of their progress.
7. Favoritism.

Notice that every single item has to do with the failure to recognize the importance of the employee. We're talking about people needing appreciation. I try to apply this principle every time I meet a person. Within the first thirty seconds of conversation, I try to say something that shows I appreciate and affirm that person. It sets the tone of the rest of our time together. Even a quick affirmation will give people a sense of value.

Treat others as you want them to treat you. Treat them as if they are important; they will respond according to the way that you perceive them. Most of us think wonderful things about people, but they never know it. Too many of us tend to be tight-fisted with our praise. It's of no value if all you do is think it; it becomes valuable when you impart it.

You Want Others to Forgive You

Almost all emotional problems and stress come from unresolved conflicts, failure to have developed right relationships with people. Because of this, many people have a deep desire for total forgiveness. A forgiving spirit is the one basic, necessary ingredient for a solid relationship. Forgiveness frees us from guilt and allows us to interact positively with other people.

Earnest Hemingway, in his short story, "The Capital of the World," tells the story about a father and his teenage son who lived in Spain. Their relationship became strained, eventually shattered, and the son ran away from home. The father began a long journey in search of the lost and rebellious son, finally putting an ad in the Madrid newspaper as a last resort. His son's name was Paco, a very common name in Spain. The ad simply read: "Dear Paco, meet me in front of the Madrid newspaper office tomorrow at noon. All is forgiven. I love you." As Hemingway writes, the next day at noon in front of the newspaper office there were 800 "Pacos" all seeking forgiveness.

There are countless Pacos in the world who want more than anything else to be forgiven. The two great marks of a Christian are that they are giving and forgiving. Show me a person who walks with God, and I'll show you a person who has a giving heart and is forgiving of others.

The unfortunate truth is that many of us, instead of offering total forgiveness, pray something like this Irish Prayer:

May those who love us, love us;
And those who don't love us
May God turn their hearts;
And if He doesn't turn their hearts,

May He turn their ankles,
So we'll know them by their limping.

People who find it difficult to forgive don't see themselves realistically. They are either terribly arrogant or tremendously insecure. Though hanging onto a grudge gives some people a feeling of satisfaction, the truth is people who do not forgive are hurting themselves much more than they're hurting others. A person who possesses this characteristic and keeps score in relationships is a person who is emotionally and sometimes physically under stress. We just aren't wired to carry all the stress that goes with carrying grudges.

A few weeks ago I met with a man who came from a devastating background. His father had suffered a stroke and his mother had been in a serious accident; both are now unable to respond to him in any way. There are areas in this man's life in which he needs and wants his parents' forgiveness, but because they are physically unable to communicate, he cannot be sure that they understand him. Every day he goes to the hospital and asks their forgiveness, but he gets no response. The situation is robbing him of any joy.

This same man has an older brother that he hasn't spoken to in over two years. It is basically the older brother's fault, and my friend wants his brother to take the first step in patching up the relationship. I challenged my friend to let God cleanse his heart concerning his relationship with his parents, and to go ahead and take the first step in making the relationship with the brother right.

The following Sunday my friend approached me after the service. He didn't say a word but gave me a great big hug. I knew what had happened and said, "You made the relationship right, didn't you?"

"Yeah, I got it taken care of," he replied—the freedom from his burden evident in his smile.

Too often people wait too long to forgive other people. Forgiveness should be given as quickly and as totally as possible. Do it now. Don't be in the position of the young man who no longer has the opportunity to communicate with his parents. Because of his procrastinatior he will never experience the joy of their forgiveness and reconciliation.

One of the most striking scenes of the last decade was Hubert Humphrey's funeral. Seated next to Hubert's beloved wife was former President Richard M. Nixon, a longtime political adversary of Humphrey's, and a man disgraced by Watergate. Humphrey himself had asked Nixon to have that place of honor.

Three days before Senator Humphrey died, Jesse Jackson visited him in the hospital. Humphrey told Jackson that he had just called Nixon. The Reverend Jackson, knowing their past relationship, asked Humphrey why. Here is what Hubert Humphrey had to say, "From this vantage point, with the sun setting in my life, all of the speeches, the political conventions, the crowds, and the great fights are behind me. At a time like this you are forced to deal with your irreducible essence, forced to grapple with that which is really important. And what I have concluded about life is that when all is said and done, we must forgive each other, redeem each other, and move on."

Do you know how to die victoriously? Quit keeping score of the injustices that have happened to you. If you are at odds with anyone, take the first step; confront the problem and ask or offer forgiveness.

I received a letter from a pastor who, along with some of his laymen, heard me speak at a conference seven years ago. The laymen all became excited about what they had learned. The pastor put up a wall of defense, though. He wasn't excited, especially when they pushed him to put the principles into practice. Finally he left the church. Recently I received a letter from him telling me that he had been bitter toward me for the past seven years. He asked for my forgiveness. Immediately I responded, assuring him that all was forgiven.

Over my years in ministry there have been hundreds of times when I've experienced strained relationships. I have had people swear at me, tell me where to go, how to get there, and offer their assistance. But I have never knowingly let them walk out the door without telling them I love them. I don't hold any grudges or carry any resentment against anyone. I cannot stress this enough: if you don't have peace, it isn't because someone took it from you; you gave it away. You cannot always control what happens *to* you, but you can control what happens *in* you.

You Want Others to Listen to You

Recently I took a break from my work and walked across the street to the doughnut shop to get a soft drink. There was a man sitting there talking to the girl behind the counter. Recognizing me he said, "Pastor, she's been listening to me all morning. I've been telling her my story." I realized how important it was to him that she was listening attentively and showed interest in what he had to say. It made him feel that he had value.

My mother was the librarian where I attended college, and each time I entered the library there would be half a dozen college girls around her desk. Mom has always had an incredible counseling ministry, not because she is such a great talker, but because she is a tremendous listener. There's a difference between *hearing* people and *listening* to them. Listening is *wanting* to hear. Mom loves people and wants to hear from them; people respond to that kind of caring.

As people gain more authority, they often develop a lack of patience in listening to those under them. A deaf ear is the first indication of a closed mind. The higher people go in management and the more authority they wield, the less they are forced to listen to others. Yet their need to listen is greater than ever. The farther they get from the firing line, the more they have to depend on others for correct information. If they haven't formed the habit of listening—carefully and intelligently—they aren't going to get the facts they need, and people will resent their decisions.

I saw a television sketch which, with some variations,

might seem familiar in many households. A husband is watching television and his wife is trying to engage him in conversation:

Wife: Dear, the plumber didn't come to fix the leak behind the water heater today.

Husband: Uh-huh.

Wife: The pipe burst today and flooded the basement.

Husband: Quiet. It's third down and goal to go.

Wife: Some of the wiring got wet and almost electrocuted Fluffy.

Husband: Darn it! Touchdown.

Wife: The vet says he'll be better in a week.

Husband: Can you get me a Coke?

Wife: The plumber told me that he was happy that our pipe broke because now he can afford to go on vacation.

Husband: Aren't you listening? I said I could use a Coke!

Wife: And Stanley, I'm leaving you. The plumber and I are flying to Acapulco in the morning.

Husband: Can't you please stop all that yakking and get me a Coke? The trouble around here is that nobody ever listens to me.

You Want Others to Understand You

How do you feel when you are misunderstood? What kinds of feelings well up inside you? Loneliness? Frustration? Disappointment? Resentment? These are common feelings when we have been misunderstood.

Peter Drucker, often called the "Father of American Management," claims that 60 percent of all management problems are a result of faulty communications. A leading marriage counselor says that at least half of all divorces result from faulty communications between spouses. And criminologists tell us that upwards of 90 percent of all criminals have difficulty communicating with other people. Communication is fundamental to understanding.

Let's capsulize what we've covered in these last few pages. You want others to:
- ☐ encourage you,
- ☐ appreciate you,
- ☐ forgive you,
- ☐ listen to you,
- ☐ understand you.

As you think about these qualities, consider how they apply to your own life. Perhaps this short course in human relations can help each of us develop qualities that we admire in others:

The least important word: *I* (gets the least amount done)

The most important word: *We* (gets the most amount done)—relationships

The two most important words: *Thank You*—appreciation

The three most important words: *All is forgiven*—forgiveness

The four most important words: *What is your opinion?*—listening

The five most important words: *You did a good job*—encouragement

The six most important words: *I want to know you better*—understanding

In life, you are either going to see people as your adversaries or as your assets. If they are adversaries, you will be continually sparring with them, trying to defend your position. If you see people as assets, you will help them see their potential, and you will become allies in making the most of each other. The happiest day of your life will be the day when you realize "we" really is the most important word in the English language.

PUT IT TO WORK

People Principles

☐ Our success, fulfillment, and happiness depends upon our ability to relate to people effectively.

☐ The key to relating to others is putting yourself in someone else's place instead of putting them in their place.

☐ Treat people the way you want to be treated:
Encourage.
Appreciate.
Forgive.
Listen.
Understand.

☐ See people as assets, not adversaries.

☐ The word "we" is the most important word in the English language.

Putting the Principles to Work:

I will apply the principles from this chapter to my relationships with people in the following ways:

1.

2.

3.

Further Study:

Bringing Out the Best in People, Alan Loy McGinnis
The Friendship Factor, Alan Loy McGinnis

2.

WHAT DRAWS OTHERS TO ME?

Understanding what people like about you and why

The greatest leaders have it—that special quality which causes people to be drawn to their magnetic personalities. Extraordinary entertainers evidence this something extra. We all have the potential to develop this quality that makes the difference between personality and *personality plus*. What quality draws others to me? We can summarize it in one word: *charisma*.

Charisma can be a difficult subject to grapple with because most people think it is a mystical, elusive, undefinable quality that you either have or don't have. However, *Webster's Ninth New Collegiate Dictionary* has given several definitions to *charisma*, and this is the one we will use, "A personal magic of leadership arousing special popular loyalty or enthusiasm."

Each one of us has certain abilities that will increase the charisma of our personality. You don't have to make a strained effort to become something that is not comfortable with your basic nature. However, if your desire is to become a people person, then you need to develop an appealing personality that causes others to respond to you.

When we examine the personalities of some of our United States Presidents, it becomes obvious why some were more successful than others in appealing to the general public. Ronald Reagan possessed the ability to convey humor, personal warmth, and relaxedness. He knew how to make others feel good about themselves. John F. Kennedy knew how to give others a feeling of hope. He exuded boundless energy and made many Americans feel important and needed. Our favorite leaders will always stand out because of the charisma factor.

Using the word CHARISMA as an acrostic, we can define the outstanding characteristics of charismatic people:

C oncern
H elp
A ction
R esults
I nfluence
S ensitivity
M otivation
A ffirmation

Keep in mind that these traits are not simply inborn; they are attainable by anyone who cares about other people and wants to develop his or her relational skills. Let's look at each characteristic in CHARISMA in more depth.

Concern—the Ability to Show You Care

Charismatic people have the ability to show concern for people's deepest needs and interests. That doesn't mean charismatic people are mushy or patronizing, but when you are around them, you sense their interest and care and leave them feeling that you are important.

Someone once asked Perle Mesta, the greatest Washington hostess since Dolley Madison, the secret of her success in getting so many rich and famous people to attend her parties. "It's all in the greetings and good-byes," she claimed. As each guest arrived she met him or her with, "At last you're here!" As each left she expressed her regrets with, "I'm sorry you have to leave so soon!"

At any gathering you will find two types of people—those who arrive with an attitude of "Here I am!" and those who possess an attitude of "There you are!" It doesn't take long to notice that people flock to the "There you are!" people.

One of my staff members, Dan Reiland, and I were talking about charisma and why so many people have trouble getting a handle on it. He gave me a simple definition, one which makes "charisma" easy to grasp: *Be more concerned about making others feel good about themselves than you are in making them feel good about you.* In other words, don't try to sell other people on you, try to sell them on themselves.

If you need to develop greater concern for others in your life, increase your exposure to hurting people. We see Jesus' sense of concern in Matthew 9:35-38 (italics added):

> And Jesus was *going* about all the cities and the villages, teaching in their synagogues, and proclaiming the gospel of the kingdom, and healing every kind of disease and every kind of sickness. And *seeing* the multitudes, He *felt compassion* for them, because they were distressed and downcast like sheep without a shepherd. Then He said to His disciples, "The harvest is plentiful, but the workers are few. Therefore beseech the Lord of the harvest to send out workers into His harvest.

Here's the sequence: Jesus went, saw, felt, and cared. It's only when we go and expose ourselves to various situations that we will see enough to develop the concern necessary to move us to action.

It's difficult to become motivated to help people without first seeing and feeling their needs. The secret is to spend time with them. Only when you go and see will you feel and do.

Help—the Ability to Reach Out

Put simply, charismatic people are helpers. They are out to see others profit; they have the gift of grace. In fact, the Greek word of gift is "charisma" meaning "gift of grace."

God has freely bestowed upon us spiritual gifts because of His grace toward us.

In Romans 12:6 we read about this further, "And since we have gifts that differ according to the grace given to us, let each exercise them accordingly." And we see in Ephesians 4:11-12, "He gave some as apostles, and some as prophets, and some as evangelists, and some as pastors and teachers, for the equipping of the saints for the work of service, to the building up of the body of Christ."

Notice in both references the emphasis on the variety of gifts and their purpose in the kingdom. It is always for other people, never for self. There is no charisma in seclusion. You can't walk into a room and have charisma by yourself!

People have problems. Many are like the beleaguered guy who, in desperation, went to a psychiatrist for help. He told the doctor, "Everytime I get my act together, the curtain falls down." He needed more than mercy and concern; he needed help. You will find that if you are adept at solving problems, that will guarantee you a following forever.

My favorite cartoon character, Charlie Brown, displayed an attitude with which many of us can identify. He and Linus were talking about their problems. Linus said, "I guess it's wrong always to be worrying about tomorrow. Maybe we should think only about today."

Charlie Brown replied, "No, that's giving up. I'm still hoping that yesterday will get better."

What can you do to help people with their problems? First of all, encourage them to face their problems. Too often people would rather flee them, fight them, or forget them.

Second, encourage them to solve their problems. Use the following acrostic to teach yourself to help people with difficulties.

T Tell them it takes *time.*

E *Expose* yourself to their problems in order to relate to them.

A *Assure* them of your confidence in them.

C *Creatively* show them how to deal with their problems.

H Offer *hope* to them through the process.

I love this old story about creative problem-solving. Mr. Myrick had to go to Chicago on business and persuaded his brother to take care of his cat during his absence. Mr. Myrick's brother was not a cat-lover, but he agreed to do it as a favor. When Mr. Myrick returned from his trip he called his brother from the airport to inform him of his arrival and to check on his cat. The brother reported in a matter-of-fact tone, "Your cat died," and he hung up.

For days Myrick was inconsolable. Then his sadness turned to anger at his brother for being so brutally honest and insensitive. He phoned his brother. "It was needlessly cruel and sadistic of you to tell me that bluntly that my poor cat had passed away."

"What did you expect me to do?" demanded the brother.

"You could have broken the bad news gradually," grumbled Myrick. "First you could have said the cat was playing on the roof. Later you could have called to say he fell off. The next morning you could have reported he had broken his leg. Then, when I came to pick him up, you could have told me he passed away during the night. Well, it's just not your style to be civilized. Now tell me—how's Mama?"

After a long pause, a meek voice on the other end replied, "She's playing on the roof."

Myrick's insensitive brother had learned that there should be a process to problem-solving.

Action—the Ability to Make Things Happen

Something exciting always seems to be happening around a person with charisma. The charismatic person has an aversion to being boring. He or she may be controversial, unusual, or entertaining, but never boring.

Be honest with yourself and evaluate how you come across to others. A young fellow in a dry church service turned to his mother and said, "Pay the man and let's go home!" That preacher obviously lacked charisma.

When evangelist John Wesley was asked why people seemed to be drawn to him, he answered, "Well, you see, when you set yourself on fire, people just love to come and see you burn."

Do you want to increase your interest with other people? Develop your creativity and your confidence. Creativity is the ability to *say* things in an unusual way; confidence is the ability to *do* things in an unusual way. Charismatic people can do both. Develop these two traits and people will stand up and take notice.

As a speaker and pastor, I always want to be fresh and exciting in my presentation. I will use humor to drive home a point but never to distract from the truth. Long after the content of the message is forgotten people will remember the creative illustration and the truth that was emphasized.

Results—the Ability to Produce

Charismatic people want to be on the winning side of life. People like being around winners and want to play on the winning team. A boy playing chess with his grandfather says, "Oh, no! Not again! Grandpa, you always win!"

Grandpa says, "What do you want me to do, lose on purpose? You won't learn anything if I do that!" But the boy replies, "I don't wanna learn anything. I just wanna win!"

Charismatic people not only want to win, they want others to win too. That creates productivity.

How does a person become productive? Find your strength and then find someone who needs your strength. Charismatic people use their strengths to help other people feel good about themselves; they are other-centered. The person who is self-centered uses his strength to dominate others.

Influence—the Ability to Lead

Leadership is influence. If something new, exciting, and interesting is happening in your life, you will want to share it. In doing so, you will influence others and they will want to follow your lead. What happens *to* you speaks of your circumstances. What happens *in you* speaks of your character. And what happens *through you* speaks of your charisma.

Do you want to learn how to be a positive influence on others? Five factors come into play:

☐ Who I am—my position or title.

☐ Where I am—my location or job.

☐ Who I know—my sphere of influence. People open doors of opportunity.

☐ What I know—my expertise. This will keep you in a position long after who you know wears off.

☐ What I do—my production, character, credibility.

Sensitivity—the Ability to Feel and Respond

Charismatic people have the ability to be sensitive to changing situations. They are adept at taking advantage of the mood, feeling, and spirit of any situation. Most people have the ability to feel something, but they aren't sure how to react to it or express it. Charismatic people not only feel it, but they know how to react and express it.

Charismatic people find a cause; that's discernment. They also voice a concern; that's courage. And they draw a crowd; that's automatic.

In the late 1960s or early 1970s I watched a television documentary on George Wallace. At the time, he was a prominent figure in American politics, perhaps because of his "redneck" philosophy over the civil rights issue. No one doubted where he stood as he proclaimed, "Segregation yesterday, segregation today, and segregation forever!" It was a perfect example of a charismatic leader playing to what that crowd wanted to hear. He was masterful at taking advantage of the prevailing mood. Because he was able to forcefully express the feelings of a certain segment of society, he became the champion of their cause.

If you are to become more sensitive, you must be willing to take a risk. Take the initiative to find a need and take action. People who are overly sensitive to the point that their feelings are always hurt will withdraw from others and never take a risk.

But the charismatic person will risk getting out of his comfort zone in order to make others feel comfortable.

Motivation—the Ability to Give Hope

The secret of motivating others is providing them with hope. People tend to feel more positive when they are following charismatic leaders. Let's take a look at some Bible people who offered hope:

☐ Isaiah, speaking of God, said, "I will do something new" (Isa. 43:19).

☐ Jeremiah talked about ". . . new law in their hearts" (see Jer. 31:33).

☐ Jesus spoke about being born again (John 3:3).

☐ Paul called a Christian a "new creation" (2 Cor. 5:17).

☐ John's vision recorded in Revelation spoke of "a new heaven and a new earth (Rev. 21:1).

Each of these dynamic leaders constantly waved hope before their people.

Do you convey hope or despair to those around you? Learn affirmation skills, problem-solving techniques, ways to verbally encourage others, and convey belief and support in others.

Affirmation—the Ability to Build Up

Charles Schwab, the successful businessman, said, "I have yet to find the man, however exalted his station, who did not do better work and put forth greater effort under a spirit of approval than under a spirit of criticism."

Everyone wants and needs to be affirmed for his accomplishments. A little boy playing darts with his father said, "Let's play darts. I'll throw and you say, 'Wonderful!'" That's what the charismatic person does for others.

We tend to become what the most important person in our life thinks we will become. Think the best, believe the best, and express the best in others. Your affirmation will not only make you more attractive to them, but you will help play an important part in their personal development.

How do we affirm others? First we need to feel good about ourselves. Then we can verbally and actively believe in others and expect them to respond positively. People are our only appreciable asset. As Christians, we cannot afford to not affirm them. If I fail to affirm a brother, we both lose.

Roadblocks to Charisma

Again, charisma is a trait or quality in our life that can be developed. It is not reserved for those who are extroverts and enjoy being in front of others. The potential to be charismatic lies within each of us, but first we must remove hindrances from the development of this important personality characteristic. What are some possible obstructions?

☐ *Pride.* A prideful person will have a tendency to look down on other people, feeling a sense of superiority. People will not follow or identify with a snobbish personality who is conscious of status and position.

☐ *Insecurity.* Insecure people are not willing to take a risk. They prefer to remain comfortable and probably, unexciting.

☐ *Moodiness.* This is an immature quality which is detrimental to personal relationships. Moody people are fickle and, thus, people who cannot be depended upon. Confidence is never built on a person who is subject to sullenness.

☐ *Perfectionism.* Perfectionism is an obsessive need to perform flawlessly. It stifles creativity and freedom and it turns people away. Perfectionists can rarely affirm themselves; therefore, it's very difficult for them to affirm others.

☐ *Oversensitivity.* Oversensitive people are constantly licking their wounds. They look inward and are not aware of the needs of others. Naturally, people don't flock around them.

☐ *Negativism.* By definition, negativism is the opposite of charisma. A person with a constant negative attitude is depressing to be around. Their personality says no to life in general. Others will avoid a person like that. There is no possibility of being a charismatic leader when no one wants to be around you.

Charisma begins at the cross of Jesus Christ. Let's take a look at Philippians 2:3-11 where we see Paul using the humility of Christ Himself as our pursuit.

> Do nothing from selfishness or empty conceit, but with humility of mind let each of you regard one another as more important than himself; do not *merely* look out for your own personal interests, but also for the interests of others. Have this attitude in yourselves which was also in Christ Jesus, who, although He existed in the form of God, did not regard equality with God a thing to be grasped, but emptied Himself, taking the form of a bond-servant, *and* being made in the likeness of men. And being found in appearance as a man, He humbled Himself by becoming obedient to the point of death, even death on a cross. Therefore also God highly exalted Him, and bestowed on Him the name which is above every name, that at the name of Jesus every knee should bow, of those who are in heaven, and on earth, and under the earth, and that every tongue should confess that Jesus Christ is Lord, to the glory of God the Father.

There is no question that Jesus was and is highly exalted. But it began with the deepest of humility. Remember: *Charisma is being more concerned about making others feel good about themselves than you are in making them feel good about you!*

PUT IT TO WORK

People Principles

☐ The key to developing charisma: Be more concerned about making others feel good about themselves than you are in making them feel good about you.

☐ Traits of a person with charisma:
CONCERN — What they show.
HELP — What they offer.
ACTION — What they provide.
RESULTS — What they produce.
INFLUENCE — What they do.
SENSITIVITY — What they follow.
MOTIVATION — What they give.
AFFIRMATION — What they share.

☐ Charisma is a trait or quality in our life that *can* be developed! The potential lies within each one of us.

Putting the Principles to Work:

I will apply the principles from this chapter to my relationships with people in the following ways:

1.

2.

3.

Further Study:

Personality Plus, Florence Littauer
Discovering Your Personality Tree, Florence Littauer

3.

HOW TO BE CONFIDENT WITH PEOPLE

Learning to feel comfortable with others

When I'm introduced to a group of people I've never met before, it only takes a few minutes to identify those who have influence over others. What is it about them that sets them apart? Is it their sense of direction—the assurance that they know where they're going? Is it an awareness that they have certain abilities? Is it their sincerity? Their past successes? Their ability to use eye contact and body language? What do they have that everybody wants?

If there is one quality you could have that would make you successful in motivating people or convincing people to follow your lead, that trait would be confidence. And if you can combine confidence with direction, guidance, past success, or some of these other motivational mechanics, you have a powerful combination. It is quite possible for a person to know where he or she is going, yet lack the self-confidence to convince others to follow along. Self-confidence carries a conviction; it makes others believe in us.

A five-year-old boy was intently working with his crayons at the kitchen table when his mother walked in and questioned what he was doing. Her son replied, "I'm drawing a picture of God."

"But honey," she responded, "no one knows what God looks like."

With great confidence the boy boldly stated, "They will when I'm done." I like that kind of positiveness.

A group of pastors were attending a conference at our church, and at the end of the first morning session they headed to the fellowship center for lunch. Several minutes later I followed, expecting that they would already be seated. Much to my surprise, all one hundred fifty of them were lined up outside the door. Then I saw why! At the head of the line stood Joel, my then six-year-old, with both hands raised, giving orders. "It will be a couple more minutes and then they'll be ready for you!" Joel had no clue what was going on, but he gave directions with the greatest of confidence and these pastors did as they were told. Confidence is contagious even if it's the confidence of a six-year-old.

The writer of Hebrews recognized the value of confidence: "Therefore, do not throw away your confidence, which has a great reward" (Heb. 10:35). Confidence is not set in cement; it's possible to lose it.

Our choice of associates will have a tremendous bearing on our confidence level. Most people fall into two categories: confidence builders and confidence shakers. If you are unsure of yourself, a confidence shaker can do you in. The following story provides a great example of confidence breakdown.

A man lived by the side of the road and sold hot dogs. He was hard of hearing, so he had no radio. He had trouble with his eyes, so he read no newspapers. But he sold good hot dogs.

This man put up signs on the highway advertising his wonderful hot dogs. He stood on the side of the road and cried, "Buy a hot dog, Mister?" And people bought his hot dogs. He increased his meat and bun orders, and he bought a bigger stove to take care of his trade. He made enough money to put his son through college.

Unfortunately, the son came home from college an educated pessimist. He said, "Father, haven't you been listening to the radio? Haven't you been reading the newspaper? There's a big recession on. The European situation is terrible, and the domestic situation is worse."

Whereupon the father thought, "Well, my son's been to college. He reads the papers and he listens to the radio; he ought to know." So the father cut down his meat and bun orders, took down his signs, and no longer bothered to stand out on the highway to sell his hot dogs.

Of course, his sales fell overnight. "You're right, son," the father said to the boy. "We certainly are in the middle of a big recession."

Confidence shakers see the negative side of everything. When they get you to buy into it, the very thing that was helping you be successful becomes your downfall.

Unfortunately, this negative process can and too often does happen in the lives of Christians. We all go through periods of testing, wondering if God really can meet our every need. With a little discouragement from a good confidence shaker, we begin to doubt His ability and our own. This can begin a downward spiral which ends in the pit of failure and frustration. Our confidence has not only been shaken but uprooted.

The positive message from Hebrews 10:35 is that our confidence has a great reward. If we keep and build on it, we will be more than recompensed. Confidence in oneself is the cornerstone to success. It is difficult for those who do not believe in themselves to have much faith in anyone else. Self-confidence breeds confidence in others, much like a boomerang which you cast out toward others only to find it comes right back to you.

Why Do You Need Confidence?

Just why do you need confidence in yourself? First of all, it will give you stability in every area of your life. Confidence equals contentment with self; contentment is knowing you have all you need for the present circumstances.

Philippians 4:11-13 provides the basis for this thought. "Not that I speak from want; for I have learned to be content in whatever circumstances I am. I know how to get along with humble means, and I also know how to live in prosperity; in any and every circumstance I have learned the secret of being filled and going hungry, of having abundance and suffering need. I can do all things through Him who strengthens me."

These verses cannot be separated because there is an absolute relationship between experiencing life's lows and enjoying its highs. The Apostle Paul is resting on the assurance that his strength is in God alone. He understood that confidence and contentment gave him stability in every situation he encountered in his tumultuous life.

Contentment is taking your present situation—whatever obstacle you are facing, whatever limitation you are living with, whatever chronic condition wears you down, whatever has smashed your dreams, whatever factors and circumstances in life tend to push you under—and admitting you don't like it but never saying, "I can't cope with it."

You may feel distress, but you may never feel despair. You may feel pressed down, but you may never feel defeated. Paul says there are unlimited resources, and as soon as you say "I can't cope," you are failing to draw on these resources that Christ has readily, by His loving-kindness, made available to you. Contentment, therefore, is being confident that you measure up to any test you face because Christ has made His strength available within you.

If the first thing confidence does is to *stabilize* you, the second thing it does is to *stretch* you. The moment that I have my foundation strong and stable, I am then in position to begin stretching. Insecure people seldom stretch because they are not willing to live on the edge of life.

Helen Keller said, "Security is mostly a superstition. It does not exist in nature, nor do the children of men as a whole experience it. Avoiding danger is no safer in the long run than outright exposure. Life is either a daring adventure or nothing."

Think about a rubber band which is totally useless unless it is stretched. When insecurity keeps us from stretching and growing, we end up with a life that is as unexciting and useless as a limp rubber band.

Confidence Helps You as a Leader

Confidence helps a leader to believe in other people. Don't we see others as we see ourselves? Show me a leader who believes in other people, and I will show you a leader who has a lot of confidence in his or her life.

An insecure leader, on the other hand, believes neither in himself or herself nor in others. Insecure people are afraid to risk building up others with compliments, because they are constantly in need of compliments themselves.

Here's a classic illustration of how confidence helps to build up other people. In the past I had the opportunity to help pastors develop lay ministry programs in their churches. Prior to the time of challenge and recruitment of laymen I would meet with the pastor to ask how many he thought would respond to the commitment. After a lengthy reflection he would give me a conservative number.

Each time, with great confidence, I assured him there would be many more who would respond. I was always right and the pastor was always amazed. Each pastor gave a lower number of responses because he mentally ranked every person according to how he perceived each one's commitment level. Therefore, he assumed a low response.

The moment you place a label on someone you begin to treat him or her accordingly. Since I didn't know these people and had no preconceived labels, I assumed them all to be quality people who would eagerly respond to the challenge. They could sense my confidence in them and responded positively. Had the pastor given the challenge, his estimate probably would have been the correct one.

A leader with confidence is a leader who brings about positive change in people. A study conducted at Springfield College in Massachusetts illustrates this point. The experiment was designed to determine the effects upon school children of having to do continuous and monotonous work without any encouragement.

The children were told to draw a detailed picture of a man. When they had finished, they were asked to draw another picture of a man. This one, they were told should be better than their first. When they had finished, they were again given the same colorless order: "Now draw another man, this time better than the last."

No matter how poor their drawings might have been, no one was scolded or criticized for his or her performance. And no matter how well the children might have done, none of them was praised or given any encouragement. They were merely told to draw another picture.

You can probably guess the results. Some of the children got angry and displayed their resentment openly. One refused to draw any more; another said he was "trapped" and called the instructor a "meanie." Most, however, just looked angry, said nothing, and continued their joyless, unrewarding toil.

Each of the drawings got worse and worse, instead of better and better, as the children had been told to make them.

People must have affirmation and praise in order to maintain a high level of performance. Withholding negative or critical comments is not nearly as important as giving positive input through compliments and praise. Again, the only people who can do this are those who feel positive about themselves. Work plus praise increases energy, but work without praise drains energy.

If you study the life of Paul, you may note he uses the word "confidence" in three distinct but related ways. Six times Paul refers to confidence in his relationship with Christ, six times to his confidence in himself, and six times he mentions his confidence in relationships with other people. There must be a balance because all three areas are related. Without confidence in Christ we could be tempted to become egocentric and cocky. Without confidence in ourselves we are defeated, powerless Christians. Without confidence in others we are suspicious and untrusting.

Paul learned this lesson and it made him a successful motivator and servant of the Lord Jesus Christ. You cannot consistently perform in a manner that is inconsistent with the way you see yourself. The price tag the world puts on us is just about identical to the one we put on ourselves. Self-confidence is the first great requisite to great undertakings.

How Can You Become Confident?
Establish your worth according to God's value system. God demonstrated our importance to Him in two great acts. First He created us in His own image, and second He—through Jesus Christ—died for our sins. God thought so much of you, believed in you, and saw you as a person of such worth, that He allowed His Son to die so that you could live. When we begin to see ourselves in light of God's actions on our behalf, then we immediately begin to have more confidence. There is nothing more humbling than the realization that if you were the only person on this earth, Jesus would have died for you. That makes you priceless.

Another way we become confident is to *focus on God and not on our situation.* Try living according to the first three verses of Psalm 27:

> The Lord is my light and my salvation; Whom shall I fear? The Lord is the defense of my life; Whom shall I dread? When evildoers came upon me to devour my flesh, my adversaries and my enemies, they stumbled and fell. Though a host encamp against me, my heart will not fear; Though war arise against me, in spite of this I shall be confident.

We can make three observations from these brief verses. First, confidence is not the result of an absence of problems. It is very clear that the psalmist encountered many problems and difficulties. He mentions his enemies, evildoers who want to devour his flesh, adversaries, and a host encamping around him.

Observation number two is that confidence is a result of trusting God *in* our problems. In the midst of his difficulties, the psalmist kept focusing on God and not on his difficult situation. "The Lord is the defense of my life."

Third, victories yesterday give more confidence for today. In verse 2 the psalmist speaks in the past tense. "When evildoers came upon me to devour my flesh, they stumbled and fell." He's talking about yesterday. In verse 3, he talks about today: "Though a host encamp against me, my heart will not fear." Confidence today is a result of victories yesterday.

Another way to develop confidence that convinces others is to *develop friendships with confident people.* The old cliché is true: Birds of a feather *do* flock together. A big man is one who makes us feel bigger when we are with him.

Many people are doomed to suffer from the "Charlie Brown complex." It seems that Charlie Brown just can't do anything right. But notice that one of his problems is the fact that Lucy is always around him. Lucy does not make it any better for Charlie Brown because she is always quick to point out the error of his ways.

On one occasion Lucy puts her hands on her hips and says, "You, Charlie Brown, are a foul ball in the line drive of life! You're in the shadow of your own goal posts! You are a miscue! You are three putts on the eighteenth green! You are a seven-ten split in the tenth frame! You are a dropped rod and reel in the lake of life! You are a missed free throw, a shanked nine iron, and a called third strike! Do you understand? Have I made myself clear?"

Do you have a Lucy around you? It's safe to say that if you surround yourself with people like her, you will have a difficult time developing a sense of confidence. Every time you start out there will be someone to remind you what you aren't, haven't been, and never will become. If we want to be confident, we must surround ourselves with confident people, people who believe in us and will be encouragers.

Another way to develop confidence is to *put a few wins under your belt.* Start with building on small successes and little by little you will tackle bigger and bigger challenges.

Recently I was listening to an interview of Jerry Coleman, the radio announcer for the San Diego Padres. He was trying to figure out why the baseball club had just blown one of their two-or-three-run leads. He commented, "You can tell by the way they're playing they have lost confidence in themselves. They have almost set themselves up for something to go wrong."

A few successful victories under your belt gives you the impetus to keep stretching your abilities. If you keep winning, you may see yourself as a no-limits person. Repeated failures produce the opposite effect. You begin to see yourself as a hopeless loser. The best way to develop rational, well-balanced confidence is to go after a few victories immediately following a failure. Don't allow yourself the luxury of wallowing in self-pity.

My son Joel and I like to play memorization card games. With the cards facing down the goal is to turn over a pair, so it is important to remember the positions of certain cards to obtain a match. One evening Joel beat me twice, 14 to 6. It never occurred to Joel that his choices could be wrong. Around the family room he rejoiced, declaring victory to all.

After two losses to Joel, I challenged his sister Elizabeth to a game. Elizabeth tends to be much less confident than Joel. When we started our first game she said, "Daddy, Joel beat you two times, didn't he?"

I replied, "Yes, he did."

She said, "The score was 14 to 6, wasn't it?"

Again I replied, "Yes, it was." And I added, "Sissy, I bet you can beat me about 14 to 6 too."

I arranged it so that I lost the first game 14 to 6. She was visibly eager to play another game which she won without my help. By this time *I* was beginning to develop a complex and lose confidence. So I got my wife Margaret to agree to play the next card game. I whipped her royally and retired a winner.

My father taught me the value of developing a confident attitude. Each night after dinner my older brother and I wrestled on the living room floor. One particular week

Larry won each match. My father noticed my sense of defeat and discouragement and told Larry that he couldn't wrestle me for one week. Instead, Dad and I wrestled nightly, and after each struggle I beat him. Dad would raise my arm high above my head and declare me the winner.

The following week he allowed Larry and me to go back to wrestling. My brother never could pin me after that. Did I suddenly acquire extra strength? No, I had acquired confidence from having some wins under my belt.

My high school basketball coach came up with the skill-building technique which he hoped would make our team more successful. He put an extra rim on the inside of the hoop, reasoning that if we could put our foul shots through the smaller basket, we would really be good with the regulation rim in the real game. I argued with the coach over the idea. I knew the guys would have difficulty sinking the ball through the smaller hoop, and the more they missed, the more discouraged they would become. I was right; they began routinely missing easy shots, because their confidence was shaken. Failure begets failure.

A great confidence booster is a personal victory list of past successes and achievements. This is a biblical concept. There are two Bible characters who practiced this: Samson, who became a total failure, and David, who became a great success.

In Judges 16:20 we see Samson's victory list: "And she [Delilah] said, 'The Philistines are upon you, Samson!' And he awoke from his sleep and said, 'I will go out as at other times and shake myself free.' But he did not know that the Lord had departed from him."

Now let's read about David's victory list in 1 Samuel 17:37: "And David said, 'The Lord who delivered me from the paw of the lion and from the paw of the bear, He will deliver me from the hand of this Philistine.' And Saul said to David, 'Go, and may the Lord be with you.' "

There are two strong similarities between these two men. They both were chosen, ordained, and anointed by God, and they were both leaders of Israel at a time when

Israel was battling against the Philistines. But this is where it stops; Samson and David also had three distinct differences. These differences made one a winner and one a loser.

The first thing we notice about Samson is that he wanted to please himself. He lived life in the flesh, depending on his own strength and felt no need to rely upon God, even when going into battle. He chose the road that always leads to ultimate defeat. Unlike Samson, David desired to please God. He knew that, left to his own resources, he was already defeated. So he called upon the Lord and went to battle with divine help. His weakness became God's strength and he was assured of victory.

Samson's alienation from God not only led to his defeat, it ended his leadership. For David, however, this episode with Goliath was the beginning of his leadership. It was the incident that brought him into a position where God could greatly use him. Victory lists should give us confidence, not cockiness.

Another way to increase your confidence is to *quit comparing yourself with others*. Comparisons always leave you found wanting. The following little story illustrates my point. A milk truck passes two cows grazing in a pasture. On the side of the truck are the words, "Pasteurized, homogenized, standardized, Vitamin A added." Noticing this, one cow says to the other, "Makes you kind of feel inadequate, doesn't it?" I think we have all known that feeling of inadequacy when we compare what we can offer with what someone else offers.

One of the surest ways to build confidence is to *find one thing you're good at and then specialize until you are special*. It could be a sport, a task, a natural ability, or a personally developed talent. Use that strength as much as you can to build your level of assurance and specialization. A successful leader knows that he helps his followers most by helping them discover their special giftedness, encouraging them to develop it, and then disciplining them to use it.

Also, *begin to develop a knowledge of people and product.* Remember that success is just 15 percent product knowledge and it's 85 percent people knowledge. Once you have knowledge of your product and of the people with whom you work, you have an inside edge on meeting their needs. That inevitably raises your confidence.

Here is a humorous old story which points out the importance of knowing who you're dealing with. A Baptist deacon had advertised a cow for sale. "How much are you asking for it?" inquired a prospective purchaser.

"One hundred and fifty dollars," said the advertiser.

"And how much milk does she give?"

"Four gallons a day," the deacon replied.

"But how do I know that she will actually give that amount?" asked the purchaser.

"Oh, you can trust me," reassured the advertiser. "I'm a Baptist deacon."

"I'll buy it," replied the other. "I'll take the cow home and bring you the money later. You can trust me. I'm a Presbyterian elder."

When the deacon arrived home, he asked his wife, "What is a Presbyterian elder?"

"Oh," she explained, "a Presbyterian elder is about the same as a Baptist deacon."

"Oh dear," groaned the deacon, "I have lost my cow."

The deacon had product knowledge; he knew his cow. But his lack of people knowledge defeated him.

What to Do with Confidence When You Have It

Now that you have all this confidence, what should you do with it? Keep refueling it! Confidence is not a constant; it fluctuates according to your success/failure ratio. We all have defeats and failures which occasionally and temporarily lower our level of confidence. If you accept the fact that you will not be outstanding in everything you attempt, you will not be devastated when your best is not good enough.

You will find that your confidence has a contagious quality. It will spread throughout your sphere of influence. The

Bible provides some interesting examples of "confidence contagion." For instance, how many giant-killers were in Saul's army? None. When Goliath defied the armies of God, they quaked with fear (1 Sam. 17:11). David, who came to bring food to his brothers, sized up the situation, went out in faith, and killed the giant. After David the giant-killer became king, how many giant-killers arose in Israel? Quite a few. They were almost a common commodity in the army under David's leadership.

Let's take a look at 1 Chronicles 20:4-8:

> Then Sibbecai the Hushathite killed Sippai, one of the descendants of the giants, and they were subdued. And there was war with the Philistines again, and Elhanan the son of Jair killed Lahmi the brother of Goliath the Gittite, the shaft of whose spear was like a weaver's beam. And again there was war at Gath, where there was a man of great stature who had twenty-four fingers and toes, six fingers on each hand and six toes on each foot; and he also was descended from the giants. And when he taunted Israel, Jonathan the son of Shimea, David's brother killed him. These were descended from the giants in Gath, and they fell by the hand of David and by the hand of his servants.

Why do you suppose there were no giant-killers in Saul's army? Surely one reason is that Saul himself was not a giant-killer. However, under David's leadership they were numerous, because David was a giant-killer. This illustrates a tremendous principle of leadership, a principle which runs throughout the Bible—it takes one to make one! When you develop confidence, those around you—friends, family, and associates—will increase in their own confidence levels. Confidence breeds confidence.

Everyone needs to be affirmed both as a person and as a coworker. It's easy to give a generic compliment such as "You're great to work with." But a comment that really means something to a person is specific and mentions a certain quality: "I appreciate your efficiency in relational skills, and this is very important to the success of the group." We don't help others by passing on empty compliments or avoiding the necessary task of sharing needed constructive criticism. Unfortunately too often we're stingy with honest praise. Build your coworkers up and encourage them by verbalizing their worth and value in front of others. Remember, praise in public and criticize in private.

Confidence can provide the momentum you need to be the person God meant you to be. It cannot substitute for character, or skill, or knowledge, but it enhances these qualities so that you can be a person who makes a difference. When you have knowledge or skill and the momentum that confidence brings, then things begin to happen in your relationships.

The largest locomotive in the New York Central system, while standing still, can be prevented from moving by a single one-inch block of wood placed in front of each of the eight drive wheels! The same locomotive, moving at 100 miles-per-hour can crash through a wall of steel-reinforced concrete five feet thick. The only difference is momentum. Confidence gives you the momentum that makes the difference.

You remember the childhood story about the train engine that did because he thought he could. Some of the larger engines were defeated when they saw the hill. Then came the little train hustling down the track repeating to himself, "I think I can, I think I can, I think I can . . . and he began to pass all the other locomotives who were saying, "It can't be done." As he got closer to the top his speed got slower and slower, but as he reached the crest, he said, "I thought I could, I thought I could, I thought I could. . . ."

The little engine made it, but not because he had more power or more skills. The little engine made it because he *thought* he could; he had more confidence. Many times we feel like little insignificant engines. But if we hone our skills and talents, then add a good dose of confidence, we can climb hills and overcome obstacles and barriers that could have stopped us dead in our tracks. Why pull off the track and stop when we can conquer those mountains with the momentum of confidence in our engines?

PUT IT TO WORK

People Principles
☐ Confidence is contagious.
☐ Contentment is being confident that you measure up to any test you are facing because Christ has made His strength available to you.
☐ You cannot consistently perform in a manner that is inconsistent with the way you see yourself.
☐ Six steps to developing confidence:
Establish your worth according to God's value system.
Focus on God and not on your situation.
Develop friendships with confident people.
Put a few wins under your belt.
Find one thing you're good at and then specialize until you are special.
Begin to develop a knowledge of people and product.
☐ When you have knowledge or skill and the momentum that confidence brings, then things begin to happen in your relationships.
☐ A leader with confidence is a leader who brings about positive change in people.

Putting the Principles to Work:
I will apply the principles from this chapter to my relationships with people in the following ways:
1.

2.

3.

Further Study:
How to Win Friends and Influence People, Dale Carnegie
Dropping Your Guard, Charles R. Swindoll

4.

BECOMING A PERSON PEOPLE WANT TO FOLLOW

Developing the qualities of an effective leader

In every age there comes a time when leadership must come forth to meet the needs of the hour. Therefore, there is no potential leader who does not find his time. Tragically, there are times when no leader arises for that hour.

Why should there ever be a time when there is a lack of leadership? And if there are not enough leaders to meet the demand, what can be done about it? Michael Korda, the author of *Power!*, was asked to draw up a list of the most powerful people in America. His findings were published in an article called, "The Gradual Decline and Total Collapse of Nearly Everyone" (*Family Weekly Magazine*, Aug. 29, 1982). Korda said, ". . . the list of movers and shakers is not at all easy to draw up. In fact, there are very few powerful figures left in American life."

"Not so long ago teachers ran their classes; generals (or sergeants) ran the Army; policemen were feared and obeyed; college presidents were respected figures, remote and awesome . . . and so on down the line. America was, in effect, ruled by authority figures."

Unless one has been asleep through the '60s and '70s it is surely apparent that all this has changed. Korda says, "It is the result of a long process, the consequence of our fear of power and authority. . . . " Two whole generations have turned against the very idea of power.

"Power, it was felt, had led to abuse. Therefore we could do without it . . . not only could, but must. Everything must be subject to the will of the people, expressed in open debate."

Lack of trust in leadership has a tremendous bearing on all types of group relationships. It is conceivable that this distrust of authority figures has spread into many of our churches. In fact, it could well be the cause of much of the upheaval which has resulted in unprecedented numbers of pastors and other church staff members being asked to leave or being summarily dismissed from their positions.

When speaking at conferences I always enjoy taking time to share with lay people as well as pastors. One active layperson, speaking of a situation in his church remarked to me, "No one seems to be in charge. No one seems to want to be accountable." Perhaps no other statement better reflects the frustration of good churchmen. They're taught to shepherd and love, but very seldom how to lead the flock.

I teach the principle of the "leadership umbrella." Imagine an open umbrella held by a hand—the hand of the leader of that organization. Under the protection of that umbrella are all of the departments of the organization. The success of each department can never, will never, rise any higher than the level at which the leader holds the umbrella. Leadership sets the standard, whether the organization be a business, a church, or a family. The higher the standard, the more effective the leadership.

What is effective leadership according to effective leaders?

☐ British Field Marshall Bernard Montgomery: "Leadership is the capacity and will to rally men and women to a common purpose and the character which inspires confidence."

☐ President Harry Truman: "A leader is a person who has the ability to get others to do what they don't want to do and like it."

☐ An outstanding leader, Fred Smith: "Leadership is influence." That is simple but profound; a person may have a position of leadership, but if he is not affecting the thoughts and actions of others, he is not a leader.

☐ From the Bible we learn that true leadership comes from serving others. And in Matthew 15:14 we read, "If a blind man guides a blind man, both will fall into a pit."

☐ My favorite leadership proverb is this: "He who thinketh he leadeth and hath no one following him is only taking a walk."

Just where have all the leaders gone? They seem to have vanished. Is great leadership a commodity of the past? No, I believe that America will again produce leaders. The fact is that our country has experienced few crises in recent history. The last period of heroic leadership was during World War II, when America found itself in tremendous turmoil. Generally speaking, the emergence of leaders conforms to the law of supply and demand. Difficult times produce men and women who will rise to meet the crisis.

The complexity of our times hinders the rise of leadership. Perhaps we have become too analytical to take decisive action. We may be spending too much time studying our problems and not enough time solving them. A good case-in-point is President Jimmy Carter. When David Hartman interviewed Tip O'Neil, retired speaker for the House of Representatives, Mr. Hartman asked who, in O'Neil's opinion, was the most intelligent President. "Unquestionably," he answered, "it was Jimmy Carter." O'Neil said Carter read and studied reams of paper on technological issues that were facing our country; he had a superior understanding of the complexities of technology. But although he was an intelligent president, he was not a strong leader. Unfortunately, the perplexing and intricate issues facing America today do not produce leaders. We are being pulled in so many different directions that it's almost impossible to unite behind a leader.

Another reason there are few well-known leaders is because of the negative reaction to authority figures following the Viet Nam war years. The peace movement and the flower children sprang up because of their disdain for war and violence. A bumper sticker reflects the attitude of the times: "Challenge Authority." There is no longer an unquestioning loyalty to those in power. Incidents like Watergate have added fuel to the fire of mistrust. America is learning to suspect anyone with authority. Recent American history has spanned twenty to twenty-five years without producing a leadership model. Interestingly enough, however, within the last few years a new sense of pride has sprung up because of Ronald Reagan's leadership style. I believe that within the next ten to twelve years we will begin to reap more directive, visionary, strong leadership types throughout our country and in our churches.

Although you or I may never attain the height of being a renowned world leader, we each have an arena of influence. We are leaders within our homes, businesses, offices, congregations, and ministries. As such, we should strive to be the most effective leaders we can be. I believe there are five nonnegotiable characteristics that every effective leader must have: a sense of calling, an ability to communicate, creativity in problem solving, generosity, and consistency.

An Effective Leader Must Feel a Sense of Calling

True leaders feel an inner urging to take their positions; they feel a sense of responsibility. I believe that the moment a father and mother see their newborn child they experience a strong calling to be godly examples to that precious new life. For the church leader or pastor, there is a specific calling from God; a deep, innate, feeling, or desire that causes him to do what he is called to perform. For the business leader, there is an urging to rise to the challenge, to take the helm and move forward.

In Isaiah 6:1-9 we find a vivid example of a man specifically called by God. In verses 1-5, Isaiah experiences a discovery of God and a discovery of himself. He becomes overwhelmed by the grandness and glory of God Himself within the holy temple, contrasted by his own unworthiness and uncleanness. People who are called discover something bigger than themselves: a mission, a challenge, a goal, or a movement that draws them into an arena.

When a person feels set apart to lead, he should also sense a strong feeling of victory. In Isaiah 6:6-7 we read, "Then one of the seraphim flew to me, with a burning coal in his hand which he had taken from the altar with tongs. And he touched my mouth with it and said 'Behold, this has touched your lips; and your iniquity is taken away, and your sin is forgiven.'" The leader experiences an assurance that he will be adequate for the work. This foretaste of victory enables them to continue on in their mission and overcome obstacles in the way.

A leader will always find his or her time. There will come times when a leader's particular gifts and talents are necessary to meet a crisis. Leaders try to use and exercise their gifts for the glory of God. They also will feel a strong desire, an urging, to be used by God. In verse 8 Isaiah is offered the opportunity: "Whom shall I send, and who will go for Us?" And then in verse 9 he exercises the desire to be used: "Here am I. Send me!"

This desire within the leader's heart is what I call the "have to" feeling. Personally, I feel a sense of "having to" declare something, point in some direction, lead others on a mission. I do not feel a sense of choice in the matter. In fact, there are times when I would prefer to sit back and let someone else take on my challenge. But when I see or feel God doing something, that "have to" feeling compels me to keep going. The followers of a true leader confirm his calling. He doesn't have to declare his calling, others do it for him.

What about the person who is not in Christian ministry? I believe God places each of us in areas where we can use our gifts and influence others for His sake. A man might be called to begin a business, for instance. He knows he is putting his money, his credit, even his credibility right on the line. There is something within him that drives him and compels him.

Perhaps you are wondering if a person can be a great leader without this sense of calling. I believe a person can be a good leader but not a great one. It sounds rather mystical but I believe God places His hand on those whom He calls to be great leaders. Everyone in leadership, however, can cultivate and enhance their leadership skills.

How do you sense that a leader is called? One clue is that called leaders have a lasting quality; they don't quit and couldn't if they wanted to. Also, the anointed people have the right answers; the God who called them equips them. There are many voices in the crowd, but the called leader stands out among all the others. He or she rises above the normal, the typical, the usual. The called leader tends to reproduce other called leaders; there is fruit in their ministry. Called leaders are relevant and speak to the times and issues.

An Effective Leader Must Be Able to Communicate

Great leaders have the ability to visually communicate their message to people. Some time ago I watched Ronald and Nancy Reagan on *Good Morning America*. Nancy was close to the edge of the stage and she fell off. Immediately people rushed to help her while the President watched. Knowing she was all right he looked at her and said, "Nancy, I told you not to fall off the platform unless I wasn't getting any applause." President Reagan was able to use an embarrassing incident as a tool to communicate. He communicated to the audience that he was in control, that he had a quick wit, and that he trusted his relationship with his wife enough to joke about her mishap.

Good communicators are able to convey a strong belief in their people; there is a very high trust factor. Again, I think Ronald Reagan demonstrated this quality as well as anyone in recent memory. Consider the following excerpt from *Fortune* magazine, September 15, 1986:

Picking competent people who are on his wave-length has also enabled Reagan to delegate more effectively than most presidents. Former Transportation Secretary Drew Lewis recounts an incident during the 1981 air traffic controller's strike that set the tone for labor-management relations throughout the Reagan era. Lewis worried that Reagan's friends, whose private planes were grounded, might urge him to back down on his decision to fire the controllers, which Lewis had recommended. So the transportation chief called Reagan to test his resolve. Recalls Lewis: "The President said: 'Drew, don't worry about me. When I support someone—and you're right on this strike—I'll continue to support him, and you never have to ask that question again.' From that day on, it was clear to me—whether in increasing the federal gasoline tax in 1983 or in selling Conrail—that once he said, 'Fine,' I never had to get back to him. I had the authority."

Some longtime Reagan associates speculate that his capacity to delegate stems from his Hollywood experience. Says John Sears, his former campaign manager: "A lot of people in political and corporate life feel that delegating is an admission that there's something they can't do. But actors are surrounded by people with real authority—directors, producers, scriptwriters, cameramen, lighting engineers, and so on. Yet their authority doesn't detract from the actor's role. The star is the star. And if the show's a hit, he gets the credit.

Every asset that you're entrusted with—whether it's money, procedures, materials, technology—all of it is depreciating. All of it is becoming obsolete. Human assets also can depreciate in value. It's literally true that in some organizations, the people are worth less—and in some cases are worthless—compared with a year ago. But human assets can also appreciate in value. People can become worth more. Those who are powerful in leadership understand that one of the key tasks of management is to find ways to grow people.

On Edison's eightieth birthday, he was approached by an interviewer who asked him which of all his inventions was the greatest. And Edison, without a moment's hesitation, replied, "The research laboratory."

I doubt his answer was fully understood by Edison's own generation. People were starry-eyed over his miracle productions—the light bulb, the record player, the improvements that made radio, the telephone, and electric motors possible. He was known by his generation as the Wizard of Menlo Park. He so transformed people's dull and drudgery-oriented lives into lives that were full of entertainment and light, possibilities and alternatives, that he was respected like no other man in American industry.

But Edison understood the secret of his great success: You can't do it all yourself. If you really want to be an uncommon leader, you're going to have to find a way to get much of your vision seen, implemented, and added to by others. The leader sees the big picture, but he also sees the necessity of sharing that picture with others who can help him make it a reality.

Ronald Reagan did this exceptionally well. He established the direction for the organization but left the hands-on management to his Chief of Staff. Reagan looked to his Cabinet and White House staff to put the flesh on major initiatives and to serve up new ideas, while he focused on big issues such as tax reform or on opinion-shaping events like the summit with Soviet leader Mikhail Gorbachev. Says Harvard presidential scholar Roger Porter, who spent five years in the Reagan White House: "He does not devote large chunks of time to peripheral issues. That is one of the keys to his success."

More than other recent presidents and many corporate leaders, Reagan also succeeded in translating his vision into a simple agenda with clear priorities that legislators, bureaucrats, and constituents can readily understand. Lyndon Johnson had his vision of a "Great Society," but his legislative agenda was too cluttered. Jimmy Carter's objectives were obscured by frequent flip-flops. In contrast, Reagan's agenda of tax cuts, deregulation, a defense buildup, and a slowdown in domestic spending was set early and pursued consistently. Independent pollster Gerald Goldhaber says that nearly 70 percent of the American people can name at least one of Reagan's four priorities. By contrast, such ratings for the Johnson, Nixon, Ford, and Carter Administrations ranged from 15 percent to 45 percent.

Reagan had the ability to put the vision before the nation. How do you transfer a vision? First you must *see* it yourself very clearly; you can't transfer something that you can't see. Then you must be able to *say* it creatively so that people understand and can grab hold of it. Finally you must be able to *show* it constantly. It must be continually placed before the followers as a reminder of the goal.

Good leaders also have self-confidence and, therefore, the confidence of others. The author of this little poem understood the value of self-confidence in leadership:

He who knows not, and knows not that he knows not, is a fool; shun him.

He who knows not, and knows that he knows not, is a child; teach him.

He who knows, and knows not that he knows, is asleep; wake him.

He who knows, and knows that he knows, is wise; follow him.

Confidence in oneself is the cornerstone. People who do not believe in themselves have trouble believing in others. Others have trouble believing in them too. Self-confidence in a leader elicits the confidence of his followers, which gives him the freedom to be a risk taker and a change agent.

An Effective Leader Is Creative in Handling Problems
Everyone faces problems. The ability to creatively find so-

lutions will determine the success or failure of each difficulty.

The Chinese symbol for crisis means danger. It also means opportunity. The key is to use a crisis as an opportunity for change. You'll never succeed if you throw up your hands and surrender. The Greek poet Homer understood the value of a crisis. He wrote, "Adversity has the effect of eliciting talents which in prosperous circumstances would have lain dormant."

Remember the story of the chicken farmer whose land was flooded virtually every spring? Even though the floods caused him horrendous problems, he refused to move. When the waters would back up onto his land and flood his chicken coops, he would race to move his chickens to higher ground. Some years, hundreds of them drowned because he couldn't move them out in time.

One year after suffering heavy losses from a particularly bad flood, he came into the farmhouse and in a voice filled with despair, told his wife, "I've had it, I can't afford to buy another place. I can't sell this one. I don't know what to do!"

His wife calmly replied, "Buy ducks."

Creativity is a trait not always admired by those who don't have it. They interpret creativity and inventiveness as stupidity and impracticality. If they see the creative person as salvageable, they will try to pull him back into the mainstream of thought. He will be told to stay busy, follow the rules, be practical, and not make a fool of himself. Traditional thinkers don't realize that creative thinkers are the geniuses of the world. Had it not been for someone's inventiveness, they might not have jobs!

Walt Disney's brother tells an amusing story about Walt's budding genius as a fifth grader. The teacher assigned the students to color a flower garden. As she walked among the rows examining the students' work she stopped by young Walt's desk. Noting that his drawing was quite unusual, she remarked, "Walt, that's not right. Flowers don't have faces on them."

Confidently he replied, "Mine do!" and continued his work. And they still do; flowers at Disneyland and Disney World all have faces.

An Effective Leader Is a Generous Contributor

The measure of a leader is not the number of people who serve him but the number of people he serves. Real leaders have something to give, and they give it freely. Anthony DeMello saw a starving child shivering in the cold. Angrily he lifted his eyes to heaven and said, "God, how could You allow such suffering? Why don't You do something?"

There was a long silence and then DeMello was startled when he heard the voice of God answer him, "I certainly have done something—I made you."

Consider the comments of William Arthur Ward of Texas Wesleyan College in Fort Worth, Texas:

> If you are wise, you will forget yourself into greatness.
>
> Forget your rights, but remember your responsibilities.
>
> Forget your inconveniences, but remember your blessings.
>
> Forget your own accomplishments, but remember your debts to others.
>
> Forget your privileges, but remember your obligations.
>
> Follow the examples of Florence Nightingale, of Albert Schweitzer, of Abraham Lincoln, of Tom Dooley, and forget yourself into greatness.
>
> If you are wise, you will empty yourself into adventure.
>
> Remember the words of General Douglas MacArthur:
>
> "There is no security on this earth. There is only opportunity."
>
> Empty your days of the search for security; fill them with a passion for service.

> Empty your hours of the ambition for recognition;
> fill them with the aspiration for achievement.
> Empty your moments of the need for entertain-
> ment; fill them with the quest for creativity.

If you are wise, you will lose yourself into immortality. Lose your cynicism. Lose your doubts. Lose your fears. Lose your anxiety. Lose your unbelief.

Remember these truths: A person must soon forget himself to be long remembered. He must empty himself in order to discover a fuller self. He must lose himself to find himself. Forget yourself into greatness. Empty yourself into adventure. Lose yourself into immortality.

It sounds like Jesus, doesn't it? Great leaders are great givers.

An Effective Leader Acts Consistently

I put this last because there are many people who are consistent but are not leaders, yet no one has ever been an effective leader over the long haul without being consistent. The moment people learn we are not dependable or responsible is the moment they will not recognize our leadership.

I recently saw a cartoon that illustrates this important principle. A young man is telling the preacher, "Being a minister must be really hard. I mean, living for others, leading an exemplary life. That's a lot of responsibility. The pressures must be tremendous! Having to set a good example . . . people watching, waiting for one false move, one sign of human frailty they can jump on! Oh, I don't know how you handle it!"

Finally the preacher sheepishly says, "I stay home a lot."

The word *being* is derived from a root meaning "to engrave." When we speak about someone's "being," we are referring to all those qualities and characteristics which identify that particular individual. "Being" may be correctly called "the signature of our soul." It is what we are. By our actions, though, it can be enhanced or diminished.

"The first key to greatness," Socrates reminds us, "is to *be* in reality what we appear to be." Jesus expressed the same idea in the Sermon on the Mount. "Beware of the false prophets, who come to you in sheep's clothing but inwardly are ravenous wolves" (Matt. 7:15).

A leader must be consistent in three areas: people—this builds security; principles—this provides direction; and projects—this builds morale. Leaders let people know where they're coming from. A recent study showed that people would rather follow a leader they disagree with than one they agree with if the latter is constantly changing positions.

The call to be a leader is a challenging one. The need for strong leadership has never been clearer. The price of leadership has never been higher. The temptations of leadership have never been greater. The hour for leadership has never been closer. Take the challenge! Remember, "in every age there comes a time when leadership must come forth to meet the needs of the hour. Therefore, there is no potential leader who does not find his time. Tragically there are times when no leader arises for that hour."

You can be the leader for your hour.

PUT IT TO WORK

People Principles
☐ Leadership is influence.

☐ He who thinketh he leadeth and hath no one following him is only taking a walk.

☐ The followers of a true leader confirm his calling. He doesn't have to declare his calling, others do it for him.

☐ Those who are powerful in leadership understand that one of the key tasks of management is to find ways to grow people.

☐ Self-confidence in a leader elicits the confidence of his followers, which gives him the freedom to be a risk-taker and a change agent.

☐ A leader must be consistent in three areas:
People—This builds security.
Principles—This provides direction.
Projects—This builds morale.

Putting the Principles to Work:
I will apply the principles from this chapter to my relationships with people in the following ways:

1.

2.

3.

Further Study:
Learning to Lead, Fred Smith
Leadership, Greatness, and Servanthood, Philip Greenslade

5.

MOTIVATING PEOPLE FOR THEIR BENEFIT

Developing the art of drawing out the best in people

At what point in life does a person learn how to be persuasive? When does he learn the fine art of convincing others that what's good for him is good for them too. Have you ever been around a newborn baby who is hungry, or needs a diaper change, or just wants to be held? It doesn't take long for that baby to persuade some adult that some kind of action is being called for! Nobody enjoys being around a red-faced, crying baby for very long.

As that baby grows older, his motivational methods become more refined. He learns when to throw temper tantrums and when to take an apple to the teacher. He learns what types of behavior get him in trouble and what types get him what he wants. This ability to persuade, which is evident from the moment of birth, should become more refined and beneficial to us and those we lead as we experience life and relationships.

Just before school the other day, my son Joel wanted to go outside and see the construction workers in front of our house. He knows them all by name, and they certainly know him! He considers himself vital to the completion of the project. When I asked him if he had brushed his teeth he said he had. Well I knew he hadn't, and because he lied to me I told him he could not go outside to watch the workers and would instead have to brush his teeth. Crying, he went to his room. Shortly, he returned looking like the cat who had swallowed the canary. "Dad," he said, "how about letting me go outside this morning and you can take away my television privileges for today?"

I said, "No, I'm sorry you cannot go outside."

He cried again and went back to his room. Two minutes later he returned with another big smile, "How about taking my computer privileges away?"

Obviously, Joel was trying to negotiate and persuade me to change my mind. He's good at it, but in case you're wondering, he did not go outside that morning!

I heard the story of a wealthy Texan who threw a party for his daughter because she was approaching the age to marry. He wanted to find a suitable husband for her— someone who was courageous, intelligent, and highly motivated. He invited a lot of young, eligible bachelors.

After they had enjoyed a wonderful time at the party, he took the suitors to the backyard and showed them an Olympic-size swimming pool filled with poisonous snakes and alligators. He announced, "Whoever will dive in this pool and swim the length of it can have his choice of one of three things: One, he can have a million dollars; two, ten thousand acres of my best land; or three, the hand of my daughter, who upon my death will inherit everything I own."

No sooner had he finished when one young man splashed into the pool and reappeared on the other side in less than two seconds. The rich Texan was overwhelmed with the guy's enthusiasm. "Man, I have never seen anyone so excited and motivated in all my life. I'd like to ask you: do you want the million dollars, 10,000 acres, or my daughter?

The young man looked at him sheepishly, "Sir," he said, "I would like to know *who* pushed me in the pool!"

The world has some misconceptions about persuasion. People have attached negative connotations to persuasion and associated it with manipulation. Actually, the Latin meaning of the word is very positive. "Per" means "through" and "suasio" means "sweetness." So, to persuade means to use sweetness to get people to do things. Effective persuasion is a result of relating, not ruling. It speaks to the heart as well as to the head. Therefore, persuasion does not make use of force or intimidation.

Getting someone to do something without convincing them it's the right thing to do is not the result of effective motivation; it's the result of intimidation. It's like the mom who told the little kid to sit down in the grocery cart at the supermarket. He kept standing up and she kept telling him to sit down. Finally she reprimanded him firmly enough that he sat down. She heard him whisper to himself as he was scrambling down, "I may be sitting down on the outside, but I'm standing up on the inside!"

When we succeed in getting people to sit down on the outside while they're still standing up on the inside, we are not persuading them; they are just accommodating us. We have neither convinced them nor have we met their basic needs.

One Man's Persuasive Ability

The following incident lays the foundation for the rest of this chapter. It is a dramatic account of the persuasive ability of Emile Zola Berman as told by attorney Morton Janklo.

> When Emile Zola Berman, the famous trial lawyer from New York, entered the Non-Commissioned Officers' Club at the Marine Corps boot camp at Parris Island, S.C. that hot, humid July night in 1956, the tension was immediate and palpable. The usually boisterous drill instructors were stunned into silence as Zuke Berman (as he was known to the legal world) strode into their sacred precincts as if he owned the place, went to the center of the room, climbed onto a table and, with steely-eyed gaze, stared out at the assembled noncoms.

The room grew silent. Then, with the skill of the great actor that he was, Berman spoke: My name is Emile Zola Berman. I'm a civilian. I'm a Jew, and I'm a Yankee from New York City. I've come down here to save the Marine Corps. If no one helps me, I'm going back to New York to resume my life. If you care about the Corps, and if you care about the truth, come see us in our quarters tonight and help us keep you proud to be Marines.

With that, he scrambled down off the table and strode out of the room as silently as he had entered it.

The occasion for this high drama was the most famous Marine Corps courtmartial in history. Sgt. Matthew McKeon—the embodiment of the professional Marine drill instructor—was on trial on the most serious charges stemming from the drowning deaths of six young recruits in his company during a disciplinary night-training exercise in the swamps of Ribbon Creek. Berman and I (then a young attorney with experience in the military justice system) had volunteered to defend McKeon.

The key to our defense to the most serious charges was to prove that what McKeon had done did not constitute cruelty against his troops but was, in fact, common practice among Marine Corps drill instructors training young men for combat.

When we had arrived at Parris Island a few days earlier, we had fully expected the drill instructors to cooperate with us in getting at the truth about combat training. What we met instead was a stone wall—set up, we learned, by the Marine Corps brass. Nobody would talk to us. We couldn't even get witnesses from other bases. Try as we would, we could not persuade the leadership of the Marine Corps or its drill instructors that the future and credibility of the Corps was at stake.

Berman's one-minute appearance and dramatic

statement at the NCO Club was his desperate effort to break through that wall of silence. "This will either make us or break us," he said to me as we left the club.

Back in our quarters, Berman went to sleep, having admonished me to sit up and wait, in case, as we hoped, somebody showed up. At about 2 A.M. just as he had predicted, there was a light tap at the window. I let in an extremely frightened young drill instructor. "I think I know why you guys are here." he said, "and I'm prepared to tell you what really goes on in these boot camps." His testimony was the break in the dam. Before we were finished, dozens of drill instructors had come forward to testify that, indeed, the march in the swamp was common practice to discipline troops and that there was nothing "cruel or unusual" about this behavior.

Zuke Berman had persuaded a group of the toughest men in the world to do what was right in the face of fear. I have taken Attorney Janklo's account of Berman's motivational ability and pinpointed the seven principles of persuasion which follow.

Know Precisely What You Are Trying to Accomplish
Before you can persuade others on any issue, you need to know just exactly what it is you want to accomplish. Zuke Berman was specific in his purposes and goals. Businessman H.L. Hunt also understood the importance of goals; he identified three steps that we must take to reach a goal. First, we must decide what we want, then decide what we are willing to give up, and, finally, go for it.

In working with pastors one of the first things I suggest is that they develop a statement of purpose in order to help them determine where they want to go. You can't accomplish anything that counts until you know where you're going. When I first formed our statement of purpose at Skyline, I asked the church board members to assist me. I posed the question: what is the purpose of this church? Twenty-two members gave me sixteen different answers. I realized that if our lay leaders didn't agree on our purpose, we would accomplish nothing great for God. We first needed to develop one statement of purpose. So we worked together, clarified our thinking, and agreed on our common purpose for the church.

There is an inspiring plaque in the Smithsonian Museum of Science. It is a statement John Fitzgerald Kennedy made in the early 1960's: "This nation should commit itself to achieving the goal, before this decade is out, of landing a man on the moon." We know what happened in July 1969; we all watched it on television. Because the president stated a definite, achievable goal, the nation enthusiastically got behind it.

In commenting on the success of the historic moonflight, Albert Siepert, Deputy Director of Kennedy Space Center, stated in 1969; "The reason that NASA has succeeded is because NASA had a clear-cut goal and expressed it. By doing this, we attracted the best of men to our goal, and we got the support of every phase of government to reach our goal." A goal is a dream with a deadline.

To give yourself a handle on establishing and accomplishing goals, keep in mind these "Five C's."

- ☐ *Consideration.* What is the needed response? That's what Mr. Berman asked himself when he asked those tough Marine drill sergeants for help.
- ☐ *Credibility.* What must I do to get the needed response?
- ☐ *Content.* What must I say to get the needed response?
- ☐ *Conviction.* How must I say it?
- ☐ *Conclusion.* What steps do I need to take to get the needed response? Now that I have said, felt, and determined to do something, what action will I take?

A lot of organizations remind me of the little girl who was riding on a bus with her father and was unsure of her destination. She asked, "Daddy, where will we be when we get to where we are going?" Better we should know where we're headed *before* we get on the bus!

Place Yourself in the Other Person's Shoes

We persuade, not from our own perspective, but from getting the perspective of others. Mr. Berman did this in his statement, "I've come down here to save the Marine Corps." He did not say, "I have an exceptional record, and I'm here to prove it to you." He immediately identified with the pride of the Marines and he therefore had their attention as well as their respect.

Be aware of the specific reasons why the other person requires persuasion and perhaps has resisted it. What is there about your goals that he resists or resents? What need or priority of his is threatened by your goals? How can you alleviate that fear? These Marines were worried that if they came forward in defiance of their superiors' policy to keep the story quiet, they might get into trouble.

Berman did not attempt to mislead the Marines by telling them there was no risk; the risk was obvious. He chose, instead, to appeal to their pride as men and as Marines. He put himself on their side and made them realize that his objective was one they shared, namely to save the Marine Corps. By putting yourself in the other fellow's shoes, you develop a sensitivity to that person's needs and can better address the issues that concern him or her. It is not always easy to do, but it's usually necessary if you're to be successful.

Recently I joined Dr. Carl George and Dr. C. Peter Wagner for a conference called "How to Break the 200 Barrier." When they assigned me that topic I knew it was a "hot button" because most churches in America are below that number. I recalled that stage in my own ministry in Hillham, Indiana. I had to be able to identify with the pastors of small churches before I could encourage them. There were three questions that I had to answer before I could put myself in their shoes. These are generic questions which you, too, can use.

First, *what do they know?* With what kinds of experiences have they dealt? If all you have is a hammer, everything looks like a nail. Have they been using one kind of tool? Ask people questions about what is important to them. Find out what is unique in their lives.

Second, *what do they feel?* Effective persuasion takes into account a person's emotions. Once the emotion is identified, steps can be taken to form a plan of action.

Bob Conklin, in *How to Get People to Do Things*, recalled the story of Ralph Waldo Emerson and his son struggling with a female calf and trying to wrestle her into the barn. Drenched with sweat, the great sage was on the brink of losing his self-control when an Irish servant girl came by. She smiled sweetly at Emerson as she thrust a finger into the animal's mouth. Lured by this maternal gesture, the calf peacefully followed the girl into the barn.

"People are like the calf," says Conklin. "You can poke them, prod them, push them, and they don't move. But give them a good reason—one of *their* reasons—a way in which they will benefit, and they will follow gently along. People do things for *their* reasons. Not *your* reasons. And those reasons are emotional, aroused by the ways they feel."

The story is told that when Michael Faraday invented the first electric motor, he wanted the interest and backing of the British Prime Minister, William Gladstone. So Faraday took the crude model—a little wire revolving around a magnet—and showed it to the statesman. Gladstone was obviously not interested.

"What good is it?" he asked Faraday.

"Someday, you will be able to tax it," replied the great scientist.

He won his point and the endorsement of his efforts by appealing to the interests of the Prime Minister. Here was an invention that represented Faraday's sweat, toil, and genius, but to win Gladstone's approval, it had to represent the British pound sterling.

The third question is, *what do they want?* People have certain needs and expectations. If they can see that what you want can also give them what they want, they will be much more open and receptive. That great motivational speaker, Zig Ziglar, frequently says, "You can get everything in life you want, if you help enough people get what they want." If we hit the "hot buttons," then people will be willing to pay the price.

Tom Hopkins writes in *How to Master the Art of Selling*, "You have to close through your eyes." He gives the example of a blind real-estate salesman who attributed his great success to the fact that he could not see the properties he sold and therefore, had to sell through the eyes of his prospects. "You must see the benefits, and features, and limitations of your product or service from your potential buyer's viewpoint," Hopkins says. "You must weigh them on his scale of values, not your own. You must close on the benefits that are of value to him." Your perspective determines your actions and reactions

> When the other fellow takes a long time, he's slow
> When I take a long time, I'm thorough.
> When the other fellow doesn't do it, he's lazy.
> When I don't do it, I'm busy.
> When the other fellow does something without being told, he's overstepping his bounds.
> But when I do it, that's initiative.
> When the other fellow overlooks a rule of etiquette, he's rude.
> But when I skip a few rules, I'm original.
> When the other fellow pleases the boss, he's an apple polisher.
> But when I please the boss, that's cooperation.
> When the other fellow gets ahead, he's getting the breaks.
> But when I manage to get ahead, that's just the reward for hard work.

Sydney J. Harris, the columnist, wrote: "Thomas Aquinas, who knew more about education and persuasion than almost anybody who ever lived, once said that when you want to convert someone to your view, you go over to where he is standing, take him by the hand (mentally speaking), and guide him. You don't stand across the room and shout at him; you don't call him a dummy; you don't order him to come over to where you are. You start where he is, and work from that position. That's the only way to get him to budge."

Expose the Problems Immediately

One of the classic parts of the speech by Zuke Berman is his opening statement: My name is Emile Zola Berman. I'm a civilian. I'm a Jew, and I'm a Yankee from New York City." To be a civilian, to be a New Yorker, and to be Jewish were really not the ideal qualifications for a defense counsel in South Carolina in a prominent Marine courtmartial in July of 1956. But by laying all of his cards on the table at the beginning, Mr. Berman knew that these possible stumbling blocks would be behind him, not down the road ahead.

When you face the potential problems at the start and get the emotions out, then you can get to the important issues. Otherwise, issues are never heard and all that is dealt with are the "yes, but's . . ." I rely heavily on this principle in leading my church. For example, just before a congregational business meeting, I send out a letter addressing all the potential problems that the church is facing at that time. The fact that the congregation knows the leader is already aware of the problems gives them confidence and peace of mind.

Always deal with the problem issues up front. This establishes a base of trust, which is necessary in any relationship. Failure to recognize and handle problems allows them to color the issues and create barriers and negative feelings. It creates a credibility gap. Count on having to deal with problems at some point. Better it be at the start, before they have the chance to fester and become insurmountable.

Be Prepared to Take a Risk

You might have to stick your neck out and make commitments that may cost you something. Mr. Berman stuck his neck out when he declared, "If no one helps me I'm going back to New York to resume my life."

Whenever you are attempting to change an opinion—whether of a jury in a homicide trial or of a friend, spouse, or parent—you're going to meet strong levels of resistance. There will come a moment when you've made your best case and you must be prepared to stand by it and take the consequences. Most people, when attempting to advance a point of view persuasively, become fearful that they will fail, and that fear is conveyed to the person they are trying to persuade.

Fear is the surest cause of failure. If you can work up your courage, as Zuke Berman did, present all aspects of your case, and walk away prepared for possible loss, you will most often be a winner. People have enormous respect for someone who says, "This is my case. I've been as honest as I know in explaining my position, and I hope that you will agree with me."

Leaders have two important characteristics: They are going somewhere, and they are able to persuade other people to go with them. Effective risk-taking leadership takes place when I sense *conviction* (the cause is right), and when I sense *confidence* (I can do it and others will help me do it).

Appeal to the Higher Vision

Most people are inherently decent and fair and they want to "do the right thing." They're not always sure, however, what fairness or rightness is, and they are often full of anxiety when forced to say yes or no. It is your job, as the persuader, to make them understand the human values represented by your position. They must be made to feel empathy for what you are trying to do so that emotionally they want to give you the response you seek. Zuke Berman did this when he said, "I've come down here to save the

Marine Corps." Those drill instructors understood that and admired his courage in taking them on.

The civil rights movement enjoyed its ultimate victory over bigotry when network news showed the dogs being loosed on the marchers in Selma, Alabama and the police crashing into the crowds with their clubs. Suddenly, people all across America understood the real effects of unfair and inhumane policies. Their emotions were aroused in a positive way, and it wasn't long before the President and the Congress felt that the public would support a strong Voting Rights Acts.

People don't buy newspapers. They buy news. It isn't glasses that are purchased; it's better vision. Women who spend big bucks for cosmetics are really trying to buy good looks. Millions of drills have been sold; yet not a single person wanted one. They were buying holes. Diet books are not sold by publicizing the evils and risks of being overweight; they're sold by ads depicting how attractive one can become by shedding a few pounds. Athletes do not go through the agony of practice and training to avoid losing; they do it to make the team and be a winner. Appealing to a higher vision is simply helping others become not only what they are capable of becoming but what they really want to become.

This method of motivation is not new. It was described profoundly by the philosopher Lao-tse 2,500 years ago, "A leader is best when people barely know he exists, not so good, when people obey and acclaim him, worse when they despise him. But of a good leader, who talks little, when his work is done, his aim fulfilled, they will say, 'We did it ourselves.' "

In the early part of the twentieth century, the same philosophy was echoed by Harry Gordon Selfridge, developer of one of the largest department stores in London. Selfridge, who achieved success by being a leader rather than a boss, said this of the two types of executives:

The boss drives people; the leader coaches them.

> The boss depends upon authority; the leader, on good will.
>
> The boss says "I"; the leader, "We."
>
> The boss fixes the blame for the breakdown; the leader fixes the breakdown.
>
> The boss knows how it is done; the leader shows how.
>
> The boss says "Go!"; the leader, "Let's go!"

Know When to Stop

The number-one reason most people lose arguments is not because they're wrong; it's because they don't know when to quit. There is a moment when you have marshalled all of the factual and emotional issues in your favor and have expressed them as best you can. If you continue to hammer away, you do nothing but build resentment in the person you are trying to persuade.

Zuke Berman could have said a lot more that night in the NCO Club. He could have talked about the attitudes of the brass, enumerated the issues in the case, talked about our suspicions that every man in the room had committed the same acts as did our defendant, or taken questions from the audience. In fact, he did none of these things because he knew, intuitively and brilliantly, that to belabor his point would weaken his position.

There is great dignity in simplicity. Most of the immortal works of literature not only have the brilliance of brevity but also the dignity of simplicity. The Lord's Prayer consists of only fifty-seven words, none more than two syllables. The Declaration of Independence, which revolutionized the thinking of the New World, can be read by a fourth-grader in less than five minutes. Simplicity is eloquent; it speaks loud and clear without insulting the intelligence of the listener.

Cover Your Topic with Enthusiasm

Occasionally there will be times when you're dealing with an issue about which you know you're right, but none of your techniques of persuasion can budge your opposition. Be enthusiastic! Columbia Law School professor, Jerome Michael, teaches his students this technique: "If you have the facts on your side, hammer the facts. If you have the law on your side, hammer the law. If you have neither the facts nor the law, hammer the table." A speech without enthusiasm is like a landscape painted entirely in shades of gray—there is form but no color. Enthusiasm alone will many times give you the edge you need.

In England there is a monument to the sport of rugby, the forerunner of America's football. The statue depicts an eager boy leaning down to pick up a ball. At the base of the statue is this inscription: With a fine disregard for the rules, he picked up the ball and ran.

The statue and inscription tell a true story. An important game of rugby was taking place between two English schools. During the closing minutes of the contest, a boy more gifted with enthusiasm and school spirit than with experience was sent into the game for the first time. Forgetting all the rules, particularly the one that says a player does not touch the ball with his hands, and conscious only of the fact that the ball had to be at the goal line within seconds if his school were to be victorious, the boy picked up the ball and, to the amazement of everyone, started the sprint of his life to the goal line.

The confused officials and players remained frozen where they stood. But the spectators were so moved by the boy's spirit and entertained by his performance, that they stood up and applauded long and loudly. This incident totally eclipsed the rest of the game's action. As a result, a new sport was born: Football. It wasn't because of carefully worded arguments and rule changes; it was because of one boy's enthusiastic mistake!

PUT IT TO WORK

People Principles

☐ To "persuade" means to use sweetness to get people to do things.

☐ A goal is a dream with a deadline.

☐ Five "Cs" in Motivating People:

Consideration—What is the needed response?

Credibility—What must I do to get it?

Content—What must I say to get it?

Conviction—How must I say it?

Conclusion—What steps do I need to take?

☐ We motivate best from the other person's perspective.

☐ You can get everything in life you want if you help enough people get what they want.

Putting the Principles to Work:

I will apply the principles from this chapter to my relationships with people in the following ways:

1.

2.

3.

Further Study:

Be a Motivational Leader, LeRoy Eims

See You at the Top, Zig Ziglar

6.

HOW TO BE A PERSON PEOPLE RESPECT

Understanding the value of your character

The headline on the front cover of *Time*'s May 25, 1987 issue contains simply two words: "What's Wrong?" I want to share a couple paragraphs from that issue's lead article, because it gives us a shocking glimpse of the moral fiber of America today.

> Hypocrisy, betrayal and greed unsettle the nation's soul. Once again it is morning in America. But this morning Wall Street financiers are nervously scanning the papers to see if their names have been linked to the insider-trading scandals. Presidential candidates are peeking through drawn curtains to make sure that reporters are not staking out their private lives. A congressional witness, deeply involved in the Reagan Administration's secret foreign policy, is huddling with his lawyers before facing inquisitors. A Washington lobbyist who once breakfasted regularly in the White House mess is brooding over his investigation by an independent counsel. In Quantico, Virginia, the Marines are preparing to court-martial one of their own. In Palm Springs, California, a husband-and-wife televangelist team, once the adored cynosures of 500,000

faithful, are beginning another day of seclusion.

Such are the scenes of morning in the scandal-scarred spring of 1987. Lamentation is in the air, and clay feet litter the ground ... Oliver North, Robert McFarlane, Michael Deaver, Ivan Boesky, Gary Hart, Clayton Lonetree, Jim and Tammy Bakker. ... Their transgressions—some grievous and some petty—run the gamut of human failings, from weakness of will to moral laxity to hypocrisy to uncontrolled avarice. But taken collectively, the heedless lack of restraint in their behavior reveals something disturbing about the national character. America, which took such back-thumping pride in its spiritual renewal, finds itself wallowing in a moral morass. Ethics, often dismissed as a prissy Sunday School word, is now at the center of a new national debate. Put bluntly, has the mindless materialism of the '80s left in its wake a values vacuum?

What is amazing about this article, which does not even mention more recent moral disappointments, is that it appeared in a secular magazine, not a Christian periodical. The world is calling attention to what I consider the biggest problem in our community today: the lack of morality and ethics. The Christian community faces an incredible credibility problem among leaders. If we don't get hold of this situation and turn it around, it will cause more damage to the church than anything else in this century.

One of the two or three life-changing books that I have read in the last ten years is *The Man Who Could Do No Wrong* by Dr. Charles Blair, a good friend, a wonderful Christian man, and the pastor of Calvary Temple in Denver, Colorado. I attended a conference in which Dr. Blair shared the story which was later revealed in his book.

He was a highly trusted pastor, a man with tremendous vision, who wanted to do something great for God. Unfortunately, and unknowingly, he hired fund raisers who did not share his ethics. As a result, he eventually found himself indicted and convicted of fraud.

Dr. Blair took total responsibility for the problem because he was the one who hired these men and trusted their methods. What makes this book so gripping is that this man, an outstanding Christian leader, straightforwardly admitted his wrong. The cover is gripping in itself as it reads, "Alarm bells should have rung when they called me the man who could do no wrong."

Dr. Blair talks about the fact that he was loved by his people, respected by the community, and had developed a sense of invulnerability. Everything he did and said just turned out right; he had the "Midas Touch." After hearing him speak and then reading his book, I was moved to understand the importance of credibility. I had an opportunity to ask him about this situation and he said, "John, I literally set myself up for a fall by bringing people around me and trusting them implicitly without checking on them."

Alarm bells should have rung, but Dr. Blair had felt no need to be on the alert. Not one of us is in a position where we can do no wrong. We should always be alert to alarm bells ringing to warn us that we may be on the edge of a potential disastrous problem.

Leaders and Credibility

As surely as every leader has his strengths, he also has his weaknesses. On a visit to Centerbury Cathedral, I had to laugh at a line of graffiti scrawled on one of the walls: "The Archbishop cheats at Scrabble." Even the Archbishop has a crack in his armour! But don't we all? The important thing is that we discover where our cracks are so we can deal with them.

Leaders are on the frontline of spiritual battle and are very susceptible to Satan's attacks. Often they are among his first victims. Leaders are exposed to pressures and temptations beyond the usual run of testing. Pitfalls face the unwary and traps abound even for the experienced. Satan knows that if he can get the leader to fall, many followers will go scrambling after.

Leaders are to live a higher standard than followers. It is a biblical principle which must be honored consistently. Leaders will be judged differently because their gifts and responsibilities are different.

Note the following triangle. It shows that followers have many options in how they live, how they spend their time, and choices they make. However, the farther up you go on that triangle, the more leadership you assume, the fewer options you have. At the top you basically have no options because you are a servant-leader. The options decrease as the responsibility increases

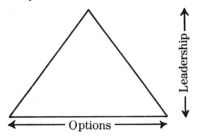

Most people do not understand this precept. Many leaders live on the principle that the more influence they have, the more options and choices they have. They begin to live as though they are above the law. James 3:1 highlights this truth: "Not many of you should presume to be teachers, my brothers, because you know that we who teach will be judged more strictly" (NIV). And Jesus in Luke 12:48 also states the same principle: "And from everyone who has been given much shall much be required; and to whom they entrusted much, of him they will ask all the more."

As leaders, we must remember that God has given us much, but He also requires much in return. We are not judged by the same standards as the world. We may sin as the world does, and we can certainly be forgiven as the world is, but it's not that easy to return to our position of leadership once we have lost credibility with others.

Some fallen Christian leaders do not seem to understand or to want to understand God's Word as it applies to forgiveness and restoration. Their attitude is that since they have asked God's forgiveness, they have every right to return to their position and privilege. Everything is *not* as it was.

When we fall, we must go through a period of proving ourselves and regaining that precious ground of credibility. Leadership is not a position which one is given but position which one earns by proving faithful.

Possibilities for failure abound, but mistakes can be avoided if the leader will listen for the "alarm bells" in his or her life. I am convinced that we do not have to step into the pitfalls. If we're looking for them, we can avoid them. Herein lies the key to success: Listen for "alarm bells." The following questions may trigger alarm bells in your own life. Consider them carefully.

Is My Personal Walk with God Up to Date?

That question should prompt a quick and positive answer. If not, you are getting too close to the edge, too close to trouble. My friend Bill Klassen asks me each time we meet, "Do you have a word from the Lord that is up to date?" or "What have you been learning recently from the Lord?" Bill isn't asking me for a history lesson; he wants to know what God is teaching me today.

You will find that leaders who are effective are leaders who are disciplined in their daily lives. A disciplined daily walk is the best protection to keep us from falling into sin.

Why is this so essential to your personal credibility? Because the Word of God convicts our hearts. Psalm 119:11 says, "Thy word have I treasured in my heart that I may not sin against Thee." It also helps us think like God. The things that we think on are the things that we become. If we are not spending time with God, we're spending that time with whatever it is that has become more important to us. When this happens we quickly become insensitive to

His Spirit and therefore, we no longer have the strength to resist temptation and do spiritual battle. It boils down to a simple fact: sin will keep us from the Word or the Word will keep us from sin.

A person of integrity is one who has established a system of values against which all life is judged. That system of values is determined by a person's walk with God. I once heard Billy Graham tell this story about a family from South Carolina who went to New York City for a vacation. They told all their friends they would attend the Broadway play, *My Fair Lady.* Unfortunately it was sold out and they couldn't obtain tickets. They were disappointed and embarrassed to have to go back home and tell their friends they missed the highlight of their trip, so they decided to do the next best thing. They picked up discarded tickets, purchased a program, and bought the musical tapes. In their motel room they learned all the songs and reviewed the program. Back home they sang and whistled the tunes to all of *My Fair Lady*'s hits hoping no one would suspect they never saw it.

When we, as Christians and leaders, begin to put on a facade, we're in trouble. When we attempt to "talk the talk" without "walking the walk," we are destined to failure. We can avoid this pitfall by keeping our walk with God close and consistent.

Am I Keeping My Priorities Straight?

Priorities have a tendency to sneak out of position when we're not paying attention. Countless numbers of Christian leaders have become "successful" only to discover the tragic price for their success was a broken marriage or loss of health. At some point along the road to success, their priorities shifted.

The first priority of any Christian should be his or her relationship with God. That means growing closer to Him, worshiping and loving Him, and being obedient to Him. The careful maintenance of this relationship is the surest safeguard against failure. One of my favorite passages is

John 21:15 where Jesus asks of Peter, "Peter, do you love Me more than these?" The question the Chief Shepherd most wants His under-shepherds to answer is not, "How much do you know about Me?" or even, "How much are you telling the world about Me?" It is, "How much do you love Me?"

Our second priority should be our family responsibilities and our third concern should be our ministry or career commitments. Paul tells us in 1 Timothy 5:8, "But if any one does not provide for his own, and especially for those of his household, he has denied the faith, and is worse than an unbeliever."

Scripture provides two illustrations of leaders who did great damage to the cause of the kingdom because they didn't keep their families in order. Both of them were judges—Eli and Samuel. I have always felt that since Eli and Samuel had a mentor-student relationship, Eli's chief weakness also became Samuel's chief weakness. That is discipleship in a negative sense.

Let's take a look at 1 Samuel 3:11-13. "And the Lord said to Samuel, 'Behold, I am about to do a thing in Israel at which both ears of everyone who hears it will tingle. In that day I will carry out against Eli all that I have spoken concerning his house, from beginning to end. For I have told him that I am about to judge his house forever for the iniquity which he knew, because his sons brought a curse on themselves and he did not rebuke them.' "

Now Samuel was a very successful judge. In 1 Samuel 3:19-20 it is said of him, "The Lord was with Samuel as he grew up, and he let none of His words fall to the ground. And all Israel from Dan to Beersheba recognized that Samuel was attested as a prophet of the Lord" (NIV).

Yet, Samuel watched the nation that he loved and led turn from the purposes of God. As God's chosen people, the Israelites were never meant to have a king; God was to be their king. But because Samuel failed to rear his sons in the fear of the Lord, Israel rejected the rule of God over them. In 1 Samuel 8:1-5 we read:

And it came about when Samuel was old that he appointed his sons judges over Israel. Now the name of his first-born was Joel, and the name of his second, Abijah; they were judging in Beersheba.

His sons, however, did not walk in his ways, but turned aside after dishonest gain and took bribes and perverted justice. Then all the elders of Israel gathered together and came to Samuel at Ramah; and they said to him, "Behold, you have grown old, and your sons do not walk in your ways. Now appoint a king for us to judge us like all the nations."

Such sober warnings in the Word of God should impress upon us the importance of keeping our priorities straight: God first, family second, ministry or career third. Only when a leader's relationship to God is right, and only when responsibilities as a family member are being properly met, can the leader be fully faithful in exercising the ministry God has given him or her.

Am I Asking Myself the Difficult Questions?

What are the critical questions? The first one is, *Why am I doing this?* Why am I spending time on this project or with these people? What are my motives? If you're doing the right job for the wrong reasons, don't count on God to bless your project.

The second question is, *How should it be done?* This deals with presumption. The danger of presumption is ever-present, especially for people called to an adventurous ministry of faith. Moses strikes the rock to produce water on one occasion and then presumes quite wrongly that this is to be God's method on a later occasion.

The third critical question is, *When should I do it?* This question deals with timing. When does God want His task accomplished? Again, aggressive leaders have a tendency to run ahead as Abraham did when he tried to speed up God's promise to Ishmael. We have a tendency to want short-term success at the expense of God's long-term will.

Am I Accountable to Someone in Authority over My Life?

In 1 Thessalonians 5:12-13 we read, "But we request of you, brethren, that you appreciate those who diligently labor among you, and have charge over you in the Lord and give you instruction, and that you esteem them very highly in love because of their work. Live in peace with one another."

You are at peace among yourselves when you are accountable to someone in authority. This is one reason why I believe in the local church. Every Christian should be a member of a local congregation and should submit to those in authority. It is very universal and very unhealthy for Christian organizations to have members on the board who are not tied in to a local church. I would be very frightened to follow someone who was not responsible to anyone. Only God Himself can handle that kind of power and authority.

My friend Ron Jenson provided me with a great idea: Stop here for a minute and write down the name of the person to whom you are accountable.

Now write out "five questions I hope no one ever asks me" on a sheet of paper. List four questions that will address your weaknesses, and then enlist the help of a Christian brother or sister who will keep you accountable in these areas. The fifth question you should seek to answer is this: Have I lied about any of the previous four questions or have I intentionally left out anything?

I believe that much of the problem of credibility in the Christian community is caused by people with power, who struggle with the same tough moral issues as the rest of the world, yet are often not accountable to anyone. Authority minus accountability equals a very dangerous situation.

Am I Sensitive to What God Is Saying to the Body of Christ?

Are you sensitive to the fact that God speaks to others too? If you can't answer an unqualified yes, you're skating on thin ice. In the checks and balances of Christian integrity, the Spirit speaks to others in the body who compliment us and make up for our weaknesses.

Paul beautifully portrays this principle in 1 Corinthians 12 when he speaks about how one member of the body is not to despise another; rather, we are to compliment each other. Not one of us has a corner on God's gift. Ask yourself this question: "Am I a listening leader or am I a lording leader?" First Peter 5:2-3 instructs us not to lord it over others. When we're more interested in telling people what to do than in listening to what they are presently doing, we are off balance.

Am I Overly Concerned with Image Building?

I am bothered by the amount of professionalism and role-playing within the ministry. Too many of us have become more interested in image-building than in kingdom-building. Pretense has replaced passion in our preaching. How we deal with the following four areas will reveal our authenticity, both in the church and outside of it.

- ☐ *Character.* Do I make decisions based on what is right or what is most easily accepted? Am I a leader or a follower?
- ☐ *Change.* Do I change my personality, speech, or actions according to the people I am with?
- ☐ *Credit.* When I do something for the Lord, do people see me or do they see my God? And do I care who receives the credit?
- ☐ *Channel.* Does God work through my life to touch others? If other lives are not changing as a result of mine, this is a good indication that the image I'm building is my own, not God's. Only if you are open, honest, transparent, and vulnerable with others can God use you to change others.

Am I Overly Impressed by Signs and Wonders?

We all seek to experience revival. But more than seeking revival, we need to seek God. Then we certainly will experience revival, healings, and miracles. But if we pursue revival for revival's sake, we're seeking after secondary results.

Luke 10:17-20 speaks to this. "The seventy returned with joy, saying, 'Lord, even the demons are subject to us in Your name.' And He said to them, 'I was watching Satan fall from heaven like lightning. Behold, I have given you authority to tread upon serpents and scorpions, and over all the power of the enemy, and nothing shall injure you. Nevertheless, do not rejoice in this, that the spirits are subject to you, but rejoice that your names are recorded in heaven.'"

God is not in the entertainment business. When He works miracles it is for one purpose only—the ultimate good of His Kingdom. A wise old minister once said to a younger one, "God can work miracles through anybody. If He made Balaam's donkey speak by a miracle, don't get puffed up if He decides to work a few through you."

When God does a great work through you, does it humble you or does it feed your ego? The appreciation and fascination for God's moving should never dim or replace our desire for holy living and righteous character.

Am I a Loner in My Service to the Lord?

Hebrews 10:23-25 admonishes us, "Let us hold fast the confession of our hope without wavering, for He who promised is faithful; and let us consider how to stimulate one another to love and good deeds, not forsaking our own assembling together, as is the habit of some, but encouraging one another; and all the more, as you see the day drawing near."

It is never healthy to be a "Lone Ranger" in service or ministry. Bring your family and your colleagues along with you. Not only is it more fun to share the joy with others, but being part of a team can provide a system of accountability. I'll never forget the first time I heard Reverend Paul Y. Cho. He stood up before more than a thousand pastors in New York and introduced one of his friends and staff members. Then he looked at his audience and said, "I bring my friend with me because I find I am susceptible to sexual temptations and he is my safeguard." The air was still and silent but we all knew what he meant. He takes someone with him so he won't mess up morally. He draws strength from a brother.

When we design our lives after the Lone Ranger concept, we are sure to suffer some unfavorable consequences. We develop a distorted perception of ourselves, our ministries, and other people. We are imbalanced and incomplete without the other members of the body of Christ and their spiritual gifts. We become irrelevant because we don't live where other people live. There is a sense of exclusiveness and an inability to relate to the real world.

Am I Aware of My Weaknesses?

To be forewarned is to be forearmed! Perhaps we should ask an even more important question: *Am I honest about my weaknesses?* Most of us know our deficiencies, but we have a tendency to try to cover them.

Take a moment now and consider areas of weakness that could cause you to become sidetracked in your life. Realize that these are the very areas in which you will be tempted. Are you tempted by opportunities simply because they may be ego-gratifying? Do you expect too much of others or not enough of yourself? Do you get your feelings hurt easily?

Besides having a weakness for chocolate, I have difficulty in keeping my schedule within the bounds of human endurance. When I allow myself to become overextended, it has a negative effect on those around me. Realizing that this is an area of personal weakness, I have set standards to help me maintain my priorities. First, each outside activity has to meet certain qualifications which I have imposed. And second, I have established a committee of three to review my schedule. Remember, though, that the first step in overcoming this weakness was to admit to myself that there was a problem.

Is My Commitment Constantly before Me?

This is supremely important if God has called you into a position of Christian leadership.

Paul says in 1 Corinthians 7:24, "Brethren, let each man remain with God in that condition in which he was called." Remember when Paul stood before King Agrippa and said, "I was not disobedient to the heavenly vision." Paul could have been tempted to give up, take other options, or yield to the persecution, but the thing that kept him on track was the vision before him.

The world continually thrusts opportunities at us which would distract us from God's call. There is nothing more tragic than when a Christian leader loses God's anointing on his life by allowing himself to become sidetracked. There is no higher violation of God's trust. For when a leader stumbles, others fall.

There have been many times when God has helped me resist temptations because I stopped and considered the harm it would do to others if I yielded.

I grew up in a church where the pastor was building a great work for God but he fell morally. Twenty years later the church is still staggering under the effects of that moral fall. That man no doubt experienced God's forgiveness, but he will spend the rest of his life wondering what he could have accomplished for God if he had not messed up. It's better not to do it than to do it and regret it.

I once heard Cavett Roberts, a great motivational speaker, say, "If my people understand me, I'll get their attention. But if my people trust me, I'll get their action." People respond quickest and most ably when the leader has credibility. If God can maintain His faith in you, so will others.

PUT IT TO WORK

People Principles

☐ Leaders are to live a higher standard than followers.

☐ Leadership is not a position which one is given. It is a

position which one earns by proving faithful.
☐ A person of integrity is one who has a system of values against which all life is judged.
☐ Authority minus accountability equals a very dangerous situation.
☐ When we design our lives after the Lone Ranger ideal, we are sure to suffer some unfavorable consequences.
☐ When a leader stumbles, others fall.

Putting the Principles to Work:

I will apply the principles from this chapter to my relationships with people in the following ways:

1.

2.

3.

Further Study:

The Other Side of Leadership, Eugene B. Habecker
The Man Who Could Do No Wrong, Charles Blair

7.

YOU CAN BE AN ENCOURAGER

Using your skills to inspire others to excellence

The key to encouragement is in knowing what gives people courage; what spurs them on to action. Too many of us take pleasure in discouraging people by pointing out their mistakes and getting excited about their failures rather than focusing on their strengths and getting excited about their possibilities.

In this chapter I want to focus particularly on "on the job" relationships. In the work force, successful managers have learned the tremendous value of encouragement. It's the greatest management principle. Why? Because you get the kind of behavior you reward. You don't get what you hope for, ask for, wish for, or beg for. You get what you reward.

It's a fact of life that people spend the most time doing what they believe will benefit them most. If they do not benefit in some way for doing the right things, they will seek other avenues of self-fulfillment. This can lead to self-destructive behavior. It's a simple thing to offer encouragement, but it can have a tremendous effect on someone's life.

When we think of organizational success, we often think in terms of dollars, cents, statistics, facts, and figures. But data and charts are nothing more than mere symbols that represent the collective behavior of human beings. Reward people for the right behavior, and you get the right results; fail to reward the right behavior and you're likely to get the wrong results.

People are encouraged to continue that behavior which brings them rewards. At home one summer we tried this principle with the kids. We set up ways for the kids to earn merit points which could be turned into money. They earned points for positive activities such as reading the Bible, Bible memory, general reading, piano practice, maintaining a clean room, and so on. Some tasks earned more points than others.

One evening I opened the front door and Joel ran to me with the news that so far he had earned 113 points. He didn't say "How are you, Dad?" "How was your day?" "It's great to see you." His greeting let me know that he was excited about success.

Behavior that is rewarded is behavior that will continue. This concept is transferable for the mom in the home, the pastor in a church, or the leader of an organization. Polls taken in the work force reveal that American workers are not giving their all; they're giving half-hearted effort to their jobs. Yet the American work ethic is still alive. If American workers deeply believe in the value and importance of hard work then why aren't they willing to give their best? The answer may be found in the reward system. Are they being encouraged by the right incentives? I believe that people withhold their best efforts when they see little or no relationship between what they do and how they are rewarded.

Rewards in Action

One Father's Day our family went to a restaurant for dinner. Unfortunately, all of San Diego chose to be at this restaurant on this particular day. Though we had a reservation there was an incredible line of people waiting to be seated. At the reservation desk stood three hostesses surrounded by a mob of unhappy people. Their stomachs were growling with hunger and it was reflected in their unsmiling faces.

After observing the scene for a few minutes I approached the desk and said, "Ladies, I have a reservation, but I see there are a lot of people here and you're under pressure. I have a large group with me today, but we want to help you. You tell me, what can I do to make your job easier? Do you want us to divide our group and go in different sections?" A hostess looked up, and smiled, and agreed that it would help for us to divide. Then I added, "I'm not going to stand here at the desk because you already have so many people pressing you. We're going to stand off to the side here and whenever you need anything just wave at me."

Every time the hostess walked by I asked her how she was doing and if there was any way we could help. Within twenty minutes we had our table. We rewarded the person who helped us. At the end of the our meal I again talked to the three ladies and said, "I know what's going to happen. Your manager is going to get a lot of complaints because I heard a lot of unhappy people." I gave them my name and telephone number and instructed them to have the manager call me if they did receive complaints. I assured them I would tell him what a terrific job they did. They smiled and were relieved. They had been rewarded for a job well done.

Once we understand the principle, we have to determine what kind of behavior deserves reward and encouragement. Look for solid solutions to problems; short-term quick fixes won't endure. Reward long-term people and programs that have been productive. At a conference I once asked the audience what success meant to them. One fellow said simply, "Success is lasting." He had a good point. Consider what will work and last over the long haul. Also identify the main factors that are most important to the long-range success of your team and communicate these to them.

In a conference at our church Josh McDowell said, "The longer I'm in the ministry and the more that I travel and see things happening, the more I have respect and appreciation for things that are long-term." That's tremendous insight. Go for quality and not quick fixes.

Qualities that Should Be Rewarded

As the senior pastor over a multiple staff I look for and reward several qualities that I feel are very important for my staff members to exhibit. I expect these things from everyone, whether they are a pastor, a secretary, a custodian, or an intern. A *positive attitude* is at the top of the list. No matter how smart or gifted a person is, if his or her attitude is not what it should be, it affects the entire team. *Loyalty* to the church, the pastor, and to one another is another crucial quality. Staff members are also rewarded for their *personal growth* because as they grow so grows their ministry. Each member of the pastoral staff is expected to reproduce his or her life into another person who could also be trained for leadership. *Creativity* is another quality that is rewarded. We want staff members who can ask the right questions and can also find creative answers and solutions.

Another behavior that I encourage is *risk-taking* instead of risk-avoiding. "Safety first" may be the motto of the masses, but it's not the watchword of leaders. No gain is ever made without the possibility of a loss. Steven Jobs, cofounder of the brilliantly successful Apple Computer, was asked how he managed to create such a flourishing new company. His reply: "We hire great people, and we create an environment where people can make mistakes and grow."

Leaders need to encourage *applied creativity* instead of mindless conformity. An organization's most important asset is not its buildings, land, or holdings. It is the creative minds within that organization. To illustrate: An employee of a company complained about the working style of a fellow worker. He said that when the guy wasn't casually walking around, he could be found sitting in his office, feet on the desk, gazing out the window. He saw his coworker's laid-back behavior as a waste of the company's money. The manager replied to his concern with: "His last idea was worth two million dollars to the company. If he only comes up with one idea like that each year, he's worth his salary."

Now I'm not advocating slothfulness, but sometimes the creative mind is misunderstood and criticized. However, if everyone is encouraged to develop their creativity within pre-approved reasonableness, the organization will benefit. Success is held in the hands of those who provide the solutions.

Determine to encourage what I call *decisive action* instead of paralysis by analysis. One pastor wanted to end a dying ministry in his church but was concerned about a small group of people who wanted to keep it going. A friend suggested, "Take it to committee. That'll kill it for sure." The purpose of any organization is to get results and that takes action, not endless introspection and meetings. Once the consulting has taken place and the reports have been delivered, it's time for a decision.

One executive summed up the importance of decisiveness beautifully: "To look is one thing. To see what you look at is another. To understand what you see is a third. To learn from what you understand is still something else. But to act on what you learn is all that really matters."

Encourage your people to work smarter, not harder. If your priorities are right—if you're working smart—your results will be fruitful. Success is not determined by how many hours you spend, but how you spend your hours. Comedian Woody Allen once remarked that showing up is 80 percent of life. Many employees behave as if showing up and being busy is 100 percent of work. Unfortunately, most of us aren't rewarded for achieving specific goals that contribute to output.

The key to working smarter is knowing the difference between motion and direction. In the final analysis, *results* are what matter; attendance and activity don't.

Encourage simplification instead of needless complication. Find and eliminate the unnecessary. Cutting the fat will produce increased efficiency which, in turn, will increase production.

Learn to ignore the "squeaking joints" and encourage the quiet, effective producers. Many times we manage by the squeaky wheel principle. The one who yells the loudest and longest is the one who gets the attention. What we need to do is look for and encourage the person who is quietly and effectively accomplishing something. You will be amazed at how fast the "squeaky wheels" catch on.

Consider this skeletal anatomy of an organization:

The *wishbones* wish somebody else would do the work.

The *jawbones* talk a lot but do little else.

The *knucklebones* knock what everyone else does.

The *backbones* actually do the work!

Encourage and reward quality work instead of fast work that is mediocre. The product needs to be something the organization can be proud of and that reflects the quality of the organization. There really are greater payoffs for quality work such as lower cost, higher output, and worker pride. Did you realize that the American car has a built-in cost factor of 25 percent because of work that needs to be redone in production due to ineffective work the first time?

Personal charisma should not be allowed to substitute for steadfastness in performance. Consistency should be recognized and rewarded. Again, look at the person who is dependable and accountable over the long haul. There are many who can make us smile and laugh but never really come through with the goods. Know the difference and encourage the producer.

Recognize and reward those who work well together. This is a key in management because none of us is as smart as all of us. There is value in creative teamwork.

Top Ten Rewards

Let's take a look at the ten best ways to reward good work. When we reward people with something that is meaningful to them, we are encouraging them as well as increasing their personal value and worth.

1. *Money.* Money does talk; it tells an individual how valuable he is to whoever pays his salary. Pay for leadership and you get leaders. Pay peanuts and you get monkeys. Did you hear about the clothing manager who turned out thousands of sweat shirts with "Money isn't everything" printed on them? He went bankrupt!

"How can I ever show my appreciation?" a woman asked Clarence Darrow, after he rescued her from legal woes.

"My dear lady," responded Darrow, "ever since the Phoenicians invented money there has been only one answer to that question."

No, money isn't the only way to show appreciation for a job well done, but it's one of the best ways.

2. *Recognition.* People need continual affirmation so they know they are meeting a need and doing it well. Lawrence Peter says there are two kinds of egotists: those who admit it and the rest of us.

3. *Time off.* If someone has worked extended hours on a special project, give them an afternoon or day off with a hearty thanks on the way out.

4. *A piece of the action.* Not all of us have the opportunity of profit sharing within a company, but we can pass on additional responsibility for work well done.

5. *Favorite work.* Reward good work by assigning people tasks they enjoy doing. Find out what they like to do best and give it to them.

6. *Advancement.* Allow only your producers to advance and move forward, not your workers. This is a biblical principle we see modeled in the Parable of the Five Talents.

7. *Freedom.* Give producers the autonomy to do their jobs in the way they feel most comfortable. Don't stifle them by trying to fit them into your own mold.

8. *Personal growth opportunities.* Reward your people with the opportunity of further career education. Provide books, conference attendance, tapes, and speakers that will enhance them.

9. *Special time together.* If you are the leader, boss, or pastor, take time to socialize over a meal in order to affirm someone's productivity.

10. *Gifts.* Your thoughtfulness in taking time to select a gift that would be meaningful shows a productive person that you appreciate him or her.

Money and recognition are the two most powerful rewards. Almost everybody responds to praises and raises!

In the final analysis, encouragement is your key to helping other people succeed. The ability to encourage is and always will be much more of an art than a science; your success depends both on your sensitivity and your skill. To use an analogy, I can only supply you with a canvas, brush, easel, pallet of colors, and a few lessons. Producing the masterpiece is up to you. You have to know how to compose the picture and blend the colors to bring about the desired effect. The same is true with people. If you are a leader you may bring together a group of highly skilled people, but that alone won't insure success. You need to know how to improve their shortcomings and build their assets by the skillful use of simple encouragement.

PUT IT TO WORK

People Principles
- [ ] Encouragement is your key to helping other people succeed. The ability to encourage is and always will be much more of an art than a science; your success depends both on your sensitivity and your skill.
- [ ] The key to encouragement is in knowing what gives people courage; what spurs them on to action.
- [ ] It's a fact of life that people spend the most time doing what they believe will benefit them most.
- [ ] Reward people for the right behavior and you get the right results. Fail to reward the right behavior and you're likely to get the wrong results.
- [ ] People withhold their best efforts when they see little

or no relationship between what they do and how they are rewarded.

Putting the Principles to Work:
I will apply the principles from this chapter to my relationships with people in the following ways:

1.

2.

3.

Further Study:
Encouraging People, Donald Bubna
Top Performance, Zig Ziglar

8.

LOVING DIFFICULT PEOPLE

Understanding and helping difficult personalities

Are you aware of the tremendous advantage frogs have over humans? They can eat anything that bugs them! Wouldn't it be great if we could consume our relational problems rather than letting them consume us! What "bugs" you the most about people? Is it inconsistency? Inflexibility? Inability to give and take? I am most bugged by people who—you guessed it—have bad attitudes. I can handle disagreements or differences of opinion, but negative attitudes really get to me.

I find that many Christian people suffer from guilt in their relationships with others. Christians are often taught that we should be full of grace. Just what does that mean? Does God expect us to get along peaceably with *everybody?* Are we the ones who must always "turn the other cheek?" Are we supposed to simply overlook other people's faults and idiosyncracies? Right relationships with difficult people can seem like an impossible standard to reach. Just what are we supposed to do?

The Apostle Paul offers this practical advice, "If possible, so far as it depends upon you, be at peace with all men" (Rom. 12:18). I would like to paraphrase that verse: Do the best you can to get along with everyone. Yet realize that once in a while you are going to have a relationship with a difficult person that may fall short of the ideal.

Right now, picture in your mind someone with whom you do not have an ideal relationship. As you continue reading, I want you to constantly call to mind this particular person. I trust you will then read about some characteristics and solutions that will help you creatively deal with the situation and be able to rise above it.

A personal inventory of the "Three P's" will help you determine your part in a difficult relationship or association.

- □ *Perspective.* How do I see myself? How do I see others? How do others see me? Our perspective determines how far our relationships will develop.
- □ *Process.* Do I understand the stages of a relationship? Do I realize there are some stages in a relationship that are more crucial than others?
- □ *Problems.* When facing difficulties in a relationship, how do I handle them?

Show me a person who sees himself or herself in a negative light and I will show you a person who sees others in a negative way. The opposite is true too. A person who sees himself positively also looks for the good in others. It's all in one's perspective.

Some people see a relationship as a series of isolated incidents, and one bad incident can break the relationship. People who think this way never develop deep relationships. Their friendships are precarious, on-again-off-again types of associations. These people run every time a difficult situation arises. They seldom, if ever, develop long-standing relationships.

Perspective and Relationships

Let's take a look at *perspective* first. I act as I see myself. In fact, it is impossible to consistently behave in a manner that is inconsistent with the way we see ourselves. Understandably, this is the cause of many marital problems. Just the other day I met with an unhappy man and his irate wife. I listened as she relentlessly spewed out bitterness and animosity toward her husband. When I confronted her with her anger and unforgiving spirit, she frantically pointed her finger at her husband and said, "I'm not the one who is angry and bitter, he is!" She transferred her negative emotions to him. She saw her husband as she herself was.

Only when we view ourselves with 20/20 vision will we be able to see other people clearly. Perspective is crucial. That's why Jesus spoke about judging others: "Why do you look at the speck in your brother's eye but do not notice the log that is in your own eye? . . . first take the log out of your own eye" (Matt. 7:4-5). He is telling us we need to deal with our own attitudes before we criticize another person.

In Matthew 22:39 we read Jesus' command to "love your neighbor as yourself." He knew that if we truly loved ourselves, we would also love our neighbor. He also knew that before we could really love our neighbor, we would need to love ourselves—not a selfish, self-serving type of love, but a deep appreciation of who we are in Christ. Most of the time our relational problems stem from the fact that we ourselves have problems or issues that haven't been resolved. It is not possible to treat another person's hurt until we have first discovered the cure and accepted the treatment ourselves.

The story of the Good Samaritan in Luke 10:30-37 illustrates this principle. The robbers who beat up the traveler used people. They stole from the traveler and saw him as a victim to exploit. The priest and the Levite were legalistic and withdrawn. They saw the beaten, robbed victim as a problem to be avoided, because they believed if they touched a dead man they would be unclean according to the Law. The Good Samaritan was a social outcast—despised, ignored, and rejected by society. He knew what it was like to be passed by and uncared for, but he also had experienced the cure. When he saw this victim, he was able to empathize with him. He looked upon him as a person who needed to be loved, identifying with the traveler's problem and sharing in the solution.

Recently I read an interesting article by Jacques Weisel

about self-made millionaires. One hundred entrepreneurs were interviewed in a search for the common denominator that bound them together. The interviews revealed these highly successful men and women could only see the good in people. They were people builders, rather than critics. Again, it is perspective that helps build relationships.

When you realize that people treat you according to how they see themselves rather than how you really are, you are less likely to be affected by their behavior. Your self-image will reflect who you are, not how you're treated by others. You will not be riding an emotional roller coaster. This type of stability will have a tremendous effect on how you feel toward and deal with others.

The key to successful relationships really gets down to responsibility. I am responsible for how I treat others. I may not be responsible for how they treat me; but I am responsible for my reaction to those who are difficult. I can't choose how you'll treat me, but I can choose how I will respond to you.

Understanding Personality Types

There are several types of difficult people, and it's helpful to identify their common traits in order to learn how to deal with them effectively. As we review these traits remember that you *can* choose how to react to them. The effect of difficult relationships—whether they make us or break us—is determined, not by the treatment we receive but by how we respond to it.

Take a look at the "Sherman Tank" personality. This label may bring to mind a person who runs over everything and anything that is in the way. These people have a tendency to intimidate others because of their "I'm-right-and-you're-wrong" attitude. They intimidate through sheer force and power; they're behavior is aggressive and even hostile. Because of the Sherman Tanks' insensitivity, people tend to battle with them. It is difficult to sit down and reason or rationalize with "tanks."

Don't lose hope; there is a strategy for dealing with the

Sherman Tanks of life. First consider this person's influence as well as the issue at stake. How important is the point being fought over, and how many people are being influenced by the "tank?" If the issue could have a direct, negative effect on others within the organization, it probably will be worth fighting over. But if it is an insignificant issue or a matter of pride, it's not worth the battle. When crucial issues arise, however, you must stand up to this personality. True, there is no easy way around these people. Be direct, because they probably don't understand tactfulness. Look at them face to face and confront the specific issues at hand. Unfortunately these people cause more pain than any of the other difficult personality types because they feel little pain themselves. As a result, they can afford to be unreasonable. What adds to the burden of dealing with these people is that, with their power to intimidate, they can pull together many allies.

Another difficult personality with whom we all come in contact is the "Space Cadet." These people live in their own worlds, walking to the beat of a different drummer. They usually do not respond to normal motivation techniques. Frustration is the overwhelming feeling I get when working with this type of person. I have learned that when working with or speaking to a large group of people, I should not be greatly influenced by this person's feedback. Probably the people you know who fall into this category, you have labeled "weird."

Consider these guidelines when working with a Space Cadet:

☐ Don't evaluate your leadership by the Space Cadet's response. In fact, don't even ask his or her opinion about something because you'll get an off-the-wall answer. Space Cadets aren't good sounding boards.

☐ It's not a good idea to place a Space Cadet in a "team ministry" position. When you need a group of individuals to pull together to accomplish a goal, the Space Cadet has difficulty pulling with other people in the same direction.

☐ Don't place Space Cadets in positions of leadership, because they won't be able to determine the heartbeat of others.

☐ Don't write your Space Cadet friend off as a lost cause, though. Search for the key to his or her uniqueness and seek to develop it. Many Space Cadets are extremely brilliant and creative; they have much to offer if you put them in the right spot. They work best when they work alone, so find an area in which they're interested and give them space to dream and create.

The "Volcano" is an explosive, unpredictable type of person who tends to be unapproachable. How do we treat them? Should we walk around them softly, or test the waters to see what kind of day they are having? It's difficult to relax around them because we don't know when the heat is about to rise. Just as the Space Cadet causes frustration, the Volcano causes tension. Those who have to work with this person can never relax; they never know what might set him or her off.

How should we handle Volcanoes when they blow up? Calmness is the key. Remove them from the crowd and remain calm yourself. They don't need an audience, and you'll be better off to keep your blood pressure down. Once you have them alone, let them vent steam. Allow them to blow as hard and as long as necessary; let them get it all out. Don't try to interrupt because they won't be hearing you. In the attempt to get the story straight, you may need to go back and ask them to repeat some details. Minimize any exaggeration and remove any hearsay that has mingled in so you can deal only with the facts and not the emotion. Then provide a soft, clear answer concerning the situation. Finally, hold these people accountable for the things they say and the people they harm.

Another person who is difficult to deal with is the "Thumb Sucker." Thumb Suckers tend to pout, are full of self-pity, and try to get people to cater to their own desires. This pouting is used as leverage to manipulate others. If things are not going their way, they can create a heavy atmosphere that is as oppressive as a rain cloud. They can do this very cleverly. Often they employ the silent treatment to get what they want.

Here's a strategy in dealing with this individual. First, make the Thumb Sucker aware of the fact that moodiness is a *choice*. This is essential. People become moody to manipulate people and gain control. They are very seldom moody by themselves. Teach them that they are responsible for the atmosphere they create, especially if they are in a position of leadership. Everybody in the world has problems; the thumb sucker has no right to add his or her personal petty grievances to the load. As a pastor, I feel responsible for creating an "up" mood for the many volunteers who work in the church, being encouraging, motivating, and positive. If you choose to lead, then you also need to choose to be even-tempered.

Sometimes it is helpful to expose the Thumb Suckers to people who have *real* problems. Perhaps it will cause them to see themselves in a different light and to have a more grateful heart and positive attitude. I knew a man who exhibited a thumb-sucking attitude, constantly feeling sorry for himself because his work was not appreciated. He was a church custodian and a perfectionist at it. The sanctuary was always spotless and the grounds were beautiful. Unfortunately this orderliness became overly important to him. It upset him when the children and adults walked across his polished floors, dropped papers on the lawn, and spilled water from the sinks. He focused his attention on himself and his clean church and lost sight of the big picture. The people coming to church to learn about Jesus should have been more important. To help him reestablish his priorities, I took him to the cancer ward at the local hospital, pointing out that these people were so sick they probably would never be well enough to come to church, and many of them probably would die without knowing Jesus. My little exercise worked; the following week there was a marked change in his attitude. He began to quit feeling sorry for himself and be grateful that he had a part in sharing Jesus.

It is important to never reward or give attention to moody people. Giving them an opportunity to publicly exhibit their negative attitudes gives them a sense of recognition. The best method of attack is to praise this person's positive ideas and actions and ignore him when he's sucking his thumb.

Thumb Suckers are subject to mood swings; they're negative only part of the time. The "Wet Blanket," on the other hand, is constantly down and negative. He is the classic impossibility thinker who sees a problem in every solution. He is afflicted with the dreaded disease of Excusitis—finding problems and making excuses.

The most difficult thing about working with a person like this is that he or she usually takes no responsibility for his or her negative attitude and behavior. It's either "the other guy's fault" or it's "Just the way I am,"—a way of blaming God. Again, don't reinforce the Wet Blanket's behavior by providing a platform from which to make excuses. Kindly but firmly point out that you have confidence in this person, but his or her present attitude is hindering progress. He needs to choose whether or not he's going to risk being positive and responsible. If he chooses to change his behavior, he'll have a cheering section. If he chooses to not change, though, your best move will be away from him.

The "Garbage Collector" is locked even deeper into the mire of negativity than the Thumb Sucker and the Wet Blanket. Garbage Collectors have surrendered the leadership of their lives to negative emotions. Oh, how they love to rehearse and replay the injuries they have suffered at the hands of other people. They nurse their wounds and hold onto their wounded ill spirits. Briefly and concisely, they stink! The fact that there is garbage in life is depressing enough, but to collect it and haul it around town in a dump truck for public viewing is downright sick.

How do you deal with these people? First confront them about the way they try to represent other people. I never allow a person to tell me "there are many others who feel this way also." I won't hear them out unless they give me names. That single requirement takes a lot of the "stink" out of their garbage because it usually boils down to just one or two individuals who have an affinity for garbage too. I challenge their statements by pinning them down when they make generalizations and exaggerations. If they have created a serious enough situation, it may become necessary to destroy their credibility by exposing them to a decision-making group. In my case, this would be the church board or the pastoral staff.

"The User" is the person who manipulates others for his or her own personal gain. Users avoid responsibility for themselves, while demanding time and energy from others to benefit their own situations. They often use guilt to get what they want. They put on a weak front in order to get people to feel sorry for them and help them out.

How do you work with Users? First, set predetermined limits on how far you will go to help them. Otherwise, they will push your guilt button and you will weaken. Remember that these people will not only take you the second and third mile, they'll take you to the cleaners if you allow them. Require responsibility from the user. Even if you feel disposed to help him, make sure he is responsible for some part of the job. Otherwise, you will wind up carrying the load while he goes on his merry way—more than likely looking for another gullible soul.

Last, don't feel obligated to users, and don't feel guilty for not feeling obligated. Most of the time a simple, firm no is the best medicine.

Perhaps you have recognized someone you know in each of these caricatures. Or maybe you're dealing with a person so difficult, he is in a category all by himself. Take heart; there are certain general rules which you can put into practice that will enable you to work more effectively with problem people.

1. Love them unconditionally.
2. Ask God for wisdom in working with them.

3. Stay emotionally healthy yourself.

4. Do not elevate people to positions of leadership in order to rescue them.

5. Be honest with God, yourself, and them.

The Process of Relationships

It's important to understand the process of relationships; specifically the stages of a relational breakdown. Let's take a look at them one by one.

☐ *The honeymoon stage* is the one we begin with. We usually have an unrealistic view of the relationship at this point. Obviously, what attracts people to each other, whether it be a business relationship, a friendship, or a romance, are their positive qualities. The excitement of finding someone who meets some need in our lives tends to temporarily blind us to their negative traits.

☐ *Specific irritation* is the stage where we begin to open our eyes and see things we don't like. Here we develop a memory bank of these negative traits. But then we also see the relationship in a more realistic light. If you look back at the early weeks of your marriage or of a new job, you will probably recall the first incident that shook you into reality—the time you realized the honeymoon was over.

☐ *General discomfort* should cause us to deal with the specific irritations that have piled up in our memory banks. We become more open, honest, and transparent about telling someone why they're making us uncomfortable.

☐ *Try harder* is a stage of development where we raise our energy level to make a success of the relationship. Unfortunately, sometimes it's very hard to separate the problem from the person.

☐ *Exhaustion* often becomes a serious problem in a relationship because we are too tired to try any longer. We tend to throw up our hands and quit at this crucial point.

☐ *Separation* is the final stage. By this time the relationship has usually been terminated with little hope of restoration. Usually, by the time this happens we are too numb to even care or hurt.

This series of stages does not have to be completed; the cycle can be broken. Most often, if the process is reversed, it happens during the stage of general discomfort. At that point it is still possible to make the decision to accept what you don't like about a person and to love that person unconditionally. As you try harder to overlook a person's faults, it becomes easier to again focus your attention on his or her positive traits.

Problems in Relationships

In most relationships it is inevitable that at some point a confrontation will take place. At this crisis point it's very important to approach the offending party prepared with the right attitude. If a confrontation is handled correctly, it can actually strengthen the relationship. If not, it can bring an abrupt, unhappy end to the relationship. In order for this not to happen, follow these six guidelines;

1. Bring in principle persons involved in the conflict. Experience has taught me that unless all persons involved come together, the whole story will never be pieced together accurately.

2. Line up the facts. Relying on hearsay evidence or "general impressions" will only invite emotion-laden rebuttals and, possibly, resentful counterattacks.

3. Never reprimand while angry. Make sure you are in control of your emotions. The angrier you are, the less objective you'll be—and the less effective your reprimand. It's prudent to delay a confrontation until you've coolly asked yourself two questions: Could I have contributed to the problem? Were there mitigating circumstances I'm overlooking.

4. Be precise about the offense. Let the person know exactly what the charge is. Don't try to soften the blow by hemming and hawing or refusing to cough up the details.

5. Get the other person's side of the story. Always give the offender the chance to explain what happened and why they behaved as they did. There may be extenuating circumstances. (Sometimes, you may even be part of them.)

6. Be sure you keep comprehensive records. The better your documentation—how the mistake came about, when it happened, who was involved, etc.—the more even-tempered and productive the reprimanding session will be.

7. Don't harbor a grudge. Once you've handed out the reprimand and administered any sanctions, don't carry around hostilities. Let that person know you consider the problem a closed book and act accordingly.

Do you remember the episode of Amos and Andy in which Andy kept slapping Amos on the chest, until one day Amos decided he had endured enough? He decided to fix Andy once and for all. Showing Kingfish some explosives tied to his chest underneath his jacket, he proudly said, "The next time Andy slaps me on the chest, he's going to blow his hand off." Poor Amos hadn't thought through the consequences of his retaliation. It never pays to hold a grudge to the point of explosion; it will do more damage to you than to the offending party.

Our ultimate goal in dealing with problems should be to present the truth in such a way as to build the relationship, not destroy it. Unfortunately, this cannot always be accomplished. If a relationship cannot stand an honest face-to-face encounter, then it probably is not a healthy relationship. In some cases, ending the relationship is the only solution, but this should be the last choice.

PUT IT TO WORK

People Principles

☐ Show me a person who sees himself negatively and I will show you a person who sees others in a negative way.

☐ Most of the time our relational problems stem from the

fact that we ourselves have problems or issues that haven't been resolved. It is not possible to treat another person's hurt until we have first discovered the cure and accepted the treatment ourselves.

☐ When you realize that people treat you according to how they see themselves rather than how you really are, you are less likely to take personally their behavior toward you.

☐ The key to successful relationships really gets down to responsibility: I am responsible for how I treat others. I may not be responsible for how they treat me; however, I am responsible for my reaction to those who are difficult. I can't choose how you'll treat me but I can choose how I will respond to you.

Putting the Principles to Work:
I will apply the principles from this chapter to my relationships with people in the following ways:

1.

2.

3.

Further Study:
The Fine Art of Getting Along With Others, Dale E. Galloway
Untwisting Twisted Relationships, William Backus

9.

HOW TO BE A PERSON WHO CAN HANDLE CRITICISM

*Learning to use confrontation
as an opportunity to grow*

Our ability to take criticism can make us or break us. No one is indifferent to criticism; it causes us to respond either positively or negatively. Just yesterday I spoke to a woman whose husband has been traumatized by destructive criticism. He has become bitter; his personality and outlook on life have turned negative.

Learning how to handle criticism was one of the most difficult lessons I ever had. I grew up in a church where the surest sign of success was a unanimous pastoral vote. At annual conference the hottest topic of discussion was the vote at the various churches. Heaven help the pastor who received negative votes! It seemed that little importance was placed on whether or not the church was experiencing growth and maturity or people were growing in their relationships with Christ. If the pastor received a unanimous vote, that was the pinnacle of his career and he was highly esteemed. It also meant that the church was spiritually in tune.

Coming from that background, I went to my first pastorate in Hillham, Indiana. At the end of the first year we had thirty-three members; the vote was thirty-one "yes," one "no," and one "abstain." That put me in a panic. I immediately called my father and asked if he thought I should resign the church. He couldn't imagine why I was so upset and laughed hysterically. Little did I realize that would be the best vote I'd ever receive in my career as a pastor! Knowing there was just one person, possibly two, who did not like what I was doing was very difficult for me to handle. Since then I've learned that if you want to do great things for God, there will always be someone who doesn't want to participate.

Taking a Positive Approach

I heard a story about a critical, negative barber who never had a pleasant thing to say. A salesman came in for a haircut and mentioned that he was about to make a trip to Rome, Italy. "What airline are you taking and at what hotel will you be staying?" asked the barber.

When the salesman told him, the barber criticized the airline for being undependable and the hotel for having horrible service. "You'd be better off to stay home," he advised.

"But I expect to close a big deal. Then I'm going to see the Pope," said the salesman.

"You'll be disappointed trying to do business in Italy," said the barber, "and don't count on seeing the Pope. He only grants audiences to very important people."

Two months later the salesman returned to the barber shop. "And how was your trip?" asked the barber.

"Wonderful!" replied the salesman. "The flight was perfect, the service at the hotel was excellent; I made a big sale, and I got to see the Pope."

"You got to see the Pope? What happened?"

The salesman replied, "I bent down and kissed his ring."

"No kidding! What did he say?"

"Well, he placed his hand on my head and then he said to me, 'My son, where did you ever get such a lousy haircut?' "

There's a saying that "what goes around comes around." This is especially true in the area of attitudes. If you are a critical, negative person, life will treat you badly. On the other hand, if you have a positive, joyous outlook, the joy you share will be returned to you.

There are two kinds of people who are highly subject to criticism. The first group are the leaders. Aristotle said it well, "Criticism is something you can avoid easily by saying nothing, doing nothing, and being nothing." Yes, one of the costs of leadership is criticism. If you're willing to stand apart from the crowd, you're putting yourself in a vulnerable position, so count on some degree of criticism.

Once after speaking about negative attitudes at a conference, I received a note that I have kept: "Realize that the guys who criticize will minimize the guys whose enterprise rise above the guys who criticize and minimize." That's what a leader does—he rises above. When you are willing to stick your neck out, someone will want to chop it off.

Don't let that threat keep you from being all you can be. Rise above it, as did the late Adolph Rupp, the former University of Kentucky basketball coach. Throughout Rupp's coaching career he experienced an uphill struggle against those who were critical of his methods. There were many who took issue with Rupp—he was difficult and sanctimonious—but it is difficult to fault the trapper with the skins on the wall. By the end of his career he had 874 victories and was the winningest coach in college basketball history.

Besides leaders the other group of individuals who are prone to criticism are the "leapers," people who leap into public eye because they are change agents. They bring unwelcome and uncomfortable change into people's lives even though it usually is for their benefit. Many years ago the medical community strongly opposed the idea of vaccinating children against disease because it was new and unknown. People who make discoveries and create inventions find it takes time for people to accept their ideas because people fear change

In the closing years of John Wesley's life he became a friend of William Wilberforce. Wilberforce was a great champion of freedom for slaves before the Civil War. He was subjected to a vicious campaign by slave traders and others whose powerful commercial interests were threatened. Rumors were spread that he was a wife-beater. His character, morals, and motives were repeatedly smeared during some twenty years of pitched battles.

From his deathbed, John Wesley wrote to Wilberforce, "Unless God has raised you up for this very thing, you will be worn out by the opposition of men and devils; but if God be for you, who can be against you? Are all of them together stronger than God? Be not weary in well-doing." William Wilberforce never forgot those words of John Wesley. They kept him going even when all the forces of hell were arrayed against him.

The question for leaders and leapers is not "Will I be confronted with criticism?" but "How can I handle and learn from criticism and confrontation?" It is possible to learn how to take criticism successfully, and the following ten suggestions can help you help yourself.

Ten Tips for Taking Criticism

1. Understand the difference between constructive and destructive criticism. You need to learn how to interpret criticism. Is it positive criticism to build you up or negative to tear you down? Someone once said that constructive criticism is when I criticize you; destructive criticism is when you criticize me.

To determine the motive behind the confrontation, ask yourself some questions. First, in what spirit is it given? Look beyond the words and determine the motives. Is the critic projecting a gentle attitude or a judgmental attitude? If your critic's attitude is kind, you can rest assured that the criticism is meant to be constructive.

Second, when is the criticism given? Times of confrontation must be shared privately, not within public view or hearing. If a person criticizes someone publically, you can be sure his or her intentions are not the best. They are out to destroy and not to build.

Third, why is the criticism given? This question deals

with the attitude of the critic. Is it for personal benefit and growth, or is it given from personal hurt? Sometimes the person who has experienced difficulties and problems will deal with others in a negative, critical way.

2. *Don't take yourself too seriously.* If you can develop the ability to laugh at yourself, you will be much more relaxed when given or giving criticism. Face it, we all do some stupid and silly things. Blessed is he who can enjoy his blunders. We are approved by God; we don't have to win the approval of others and look good in their eyes. We are not perfect people. Too many of us take ourselves too seriously and God not seriously enough.

"Life at St. Bashan's" cartoon strip portrayed a pastor who was forced to learn how to handle criticism. A parishoner approaches the pastor after the service and says, "Reverend, I want you to know that wasn't one of your better sermons."

Openly the pastor responds with, "And Bill, I want you to know I'm grateful for constructive criticism." In the next frame the pastor walks into the study, locks the door, and then falls to his knees with a cry, "Augggghhh!"

We've done that, haven't we? Outwardly we appear to appreciate the words, but in private we fall apart emotionally, becoming angry, vindictive, or deeply hurt.

3. *Look beyond the criticism and see the critic.* When someone comes to me with news about another person, I am more interested in the person who said it than what was said. In fact, that's one of my first questions: *Who* said it? *Who* told you that? When I find out who the perpetrator is, I know whether or not to listen. I will either straighten up and take it seriously or I will think to myself, "There they go again."

Keep in mind certain considerations regarding your critic: First, is it someone whose character you respect? Adverse criticism from a wise man is more to be desired than the enthusiastic approval of a fool. Second, is this person frequently critical? Is criticism a pattern? If so, don't place too much value in what they say. Possibly it's a way to get attention. Criticism from a positive person, on the other hand, probably deserves your attention.

There is a story about a twelve-year-old boy who in all of his twelve years had never spoken. After being served oatmeal for breakfast several times in a row a miracle happened! To everyone's shock, he yelled, "Yuck, I hate oatmeal."

His mother was overwhelmed. She ran across the room and threw her arms around his neck. "For twelve long years your father and I were convinced you couldn't talk!" she cried. "Why haven't you ever spoken to us?"

Bluntly the boy explained, "Up till now, everything's been OK." I'm not sure if she kept serving him oatmeal to keep him complaining, but this boy knew how to be heard.

Finally, ask yourself this question: Does the critic sincerely want to help me? Is he or she on your team, believing the best in you, desiring to help? Remember that people who are busy rowing seldom have time to rock the boat.

4. *Watch your own attitude toward the critic.* A negative attitude toward criticism can be more destructive than the criticism itself. Remember, a chip on the shoulder indicates wood higher up! The late Herman Hickman, great football coach at Tennessee, Army, and Yale, said, "When you are being run out of town, get to the head of the line and look as though you are leading the parade."

First Peter 2:21-23 provides the right attitude toward criticism:

> For you have been called for this purpose, since Christ also suffered for you, leaving you an example for you to follow in His steps, who committed no sin, nor was any deceit found in His mouth; and while being reviled, He did not revile in return; while suffering, He uttered no threats, but kept entrusting Himself to Him who judges righteously."

Could it be that a poor attitude reveals the fact that we have trusted in ourselves, rather than in God who knows the entire situation? If we are trusting Him and are obedient, we can expect some criticism. He often calls us to take an unpopular stand. He has also called us to love those who are critical of us.

5. *Realize that good people get criticized.* Jesus, whose motives were pure and character was spotless, was called a glutton (Matt. 11:19); a winebibber (Luke 7:34); a Samaritan (John 8:48); and a friend of sinners (Matt. 11:19 and Mark 2:16). If our lives are Christlike we can expect criticism. In fact, there are times when we should see criticism from the world as verification that our lives have been changed. A person whose mind is polluted and whose vision is not clear cannot understand or interpret behavior based on obedience to God. So if you're living on a higher plane than the world, expect some criticism.

6. *Keep physically and spiritually in shape.* Physical exhaustion has a tremendous effect on the way we act and react; it distorts the way we see and handle life. Recently Margaret and I were returning home from a long trip, and after being up many hours and hassling with several airline connections, we were both physically wiped out. Realizing that any attempts to communicate could put us over the edge, Margaret proposed that we each bury our face in a book. It worked. By the time the plane landed in San Diego, we were not exactly alert but we were still friends. It's a simple fact of life: These minds and bodies need rest.

Elijah succumbed to opposition when he was in a state of weariness. Jezebel was a firecracker, and her opposition sapped the preacher's strength. Elijah complained, "It is enough, now, O Lord, take away my life; for I am no better than my fathers" (1 Kings 19:4). Elijah was completely shaken. Watch weariness because Satan will take advantage. When we become overly tired, we become overly critical, and at the same time we are less able to handle criticism from others.

7. *Don't just see the critic; see if there's a crowd.* The following story illustrates this point.

Mrs. Jones had invited a great and well-known violinist

to entertain at her afternoon tea. When it was all over, everyone crowded around the musician.

"I've got to be honest with you," said one of the guests, "I think your performance was absolutely terrible."

Hearing his criticism, the hostess interposed: "Don't pay any attention to him. He doesn't know what he's talking about. He only repeats what he hears everyone else say."

I'm suggesting that you expand your vision; go beyond the critic and see if he has a cheering section. Consider the possibility that you are hearing the same criticism from several people. If this is the case, and the critics are reliable, you need to realize that you have a challenge to work on. If, on the other hand, you're dealing with a pocket group of negative people, your challenge is to not be affected by them.

George Bernard Shaw, the Irish playwright, certainly had his critics, but he knew how to handle them. After one opening, a critic voiced his displeasure. He said, "It's rotten! It's rotten!" To which Shaw replied, "I agree with you perfectly, but what are we two against so many!"

8. *Wait for time to prove them wrong.* Time is your best ally; it allows you to prove yourself right. Often, as events unfold, the cause for criticism is eliminated and you will be vindicated. You may be thinking, "Easy for you to say, Maxwell, you're not where I am." But I've been there many times. If you know your action or decision was right, hang in there. Time will prove you out.

Abraham Lincoln, the most loved president of the United States, was also the most criticized president. Probably no politician in history had worse things said about him. Here's how the *Chicago Times* in 1865 evaluated Lincoln's Gettysburg Address the day after he delivered it: "The cheek of every American must tingle with shame as he reads the silly, flat, and dish-watery utterances of a man who has been pointed out to intelligent foreigners as President of the United States." Time, of course, has proved this scathing criticism wrong.

9. *Surround yourself with positive people.* When you

have optional time, spend it with people who will build you up. Enough quality time with positive people will minimize the effect of negative criticism. It will also discourage you from being critical. When a hawk is attacked by crows, he does not counterattack. Instead, he soars higher and higher in ever widening circles until the pests leave him alone. Circle above your adversaries rather than battle with them. If your positive attitude has any effect on negative people, it will be because of your example, not your defensiveness. So rise above them. It really is hard to soar like an eagle if you identify with turkeys!

10. Concentrate on your mission—change your mistakes. Most people do exactly the opposite—they change their mission and concentrate on their mistakes. If you run from your task each time you make a mistake, you will never accomplish anything. You will always be in a state of frustration and defeat. The only real mistakes in life are the mistakes from which we learn nothing. So instead of dwelling on them, count on making them, learning from them, and moving on to finish the job. There's an Arabian proverb that says if you stop every time a dog barks, your road will never end. Don't let your mistakes become roadblocks; make them building blocks.

In order to build strong relationships you need to know how to take criticism gracefully, but there are also times when you will have to be the critic. It is possible to confront without ruining a relationship, but use caution, because careless confrontation can be devastating. Before you confront, check yourself in the following areas.

Ten Tips for Giving Criticism

1. Check your motive. The goal of confrontation should be to help, not to humiliate. Three key questions will help expose your true motives. First, ask yourself, *Would I criticize this if it were not a personal matter?* Sometimes we react differently when we are emotionally or personally involved. Here's what I mean:

Sluggo: "That new kid in school is a big fat-head!"

Nancy: "You shouldn't call people names like that. I never call people names."

Sluggo: "Well, I just got mad when he said you were silly looking."

Nancy: "What else did that big fat-head say?"

Second, ask yourself, *Will criticism make me look better?* Cutting someone down to boost yourself up is the lowest form of ego gratification. It's the sign of a very insecure person. Remember that it isn't necessary to blow out another person's light to let your own shine.

Third, ask yourself, *Does this criticism bring pain or pleasure to me?* When it is painful for you to criticize others, you're probably safe in doing it. If you get the slightest bit of pleasure out of doing it, you should hold your tongue.

2. *Make sure the issue is worthy of criticism.* To whom does it really matter? Sometimes our pride causes us to engage in skirmishes that need never happen. Continual, petty criticism is the mark of a small mind; you have to be little to belittle. The secret to not letting yourself be distracted and needled by insignificant issues is to keep your head up and your eyes on the goal.

3 *Be specific.* When you confront you must be tactfully explicit. Say exactly what you mean and provide examples to back yourself up.

I once had a staff person who had great difficulty confronting; he hated to make people face up to areas in which they needed to change. On one particular occasion I coached him. He rehearsed with me everything he was going to say to the individuals in question. After the confrontation I asked him how it went. He assured me everything went smoothly and there were no problems; in fact, he said the people did not even question him. At that moment I knew something had gone wrong. Total acquiescence is not a normal reaction to honest confrontation. Two days later the truth came out. One of the individuals said to me, "The other day we spent thirty minutes with Pastor So-and-so, but we have no idea what he was trying to tell us." The pastor had spent half an hour dancing around the issue without ever addressing it. He would have been better off to have left it alone.

If you can't be specific, don't confront. People can usually tell when you're skirting an issue and will not respect you for it.

4. *Don't undermine the person's self-confidence.* Try to find at least one area in which you can praise the person before you expose the problem. Stay away from all-inclusive statements like, "You always . . ." or "You never. . . ." Assure them that you have confidence in them and their ability to handle the situation correctly.

5. *Don't compare one person with another.* Deal with people on an individual basis. Comparisons always cause resentment and resentment causes hostility. There's no need to create a bigger problem than the one you already have, so why arouse heated emotions? If you stick to the facts, you'll be less likely to put the person on the defensive.

6. *Be creative or don't confront.* Will Rogers said, "There is nothing as easy as denouncing. It doesn't take much to see something is wrong, but it does take some eyesight to see what will put it right again."

Look beyond the problem and see if you can help find some solutions. For most of us it's much easier to be critical than to be creative. But unless you're willing to help to some degree in turning the situation around, you're not ready to comment on the problem.

7. *Attack the problem not the person.* Deal with the issue at hand. When a confrontation becomes a personal attack, you destroy your own credibility and find yourself in a no-win situation. The expected outcome of a confrontation should be that the offender leave with a clear understanding of the problem and the hope that he can turn it around.

8. *Confront when the time is right.* The right time is just as soon as you know something is wrong. When you've completed your homework then you're prepared. Sometimes people tell me about their relationship problems and

ask me for advice. The scenario is always the same and so is my advice: You cannot escape the need to talk to the person. When you wait too long you lose the opportune moment and the issue becomes history. When you confront the person in a timely fashion you are better able to keep the facts straight and use the incident as an opportunity to help the person grow.

9. Look at yourself before looking at others. Instead of putting others in their place, put yourself in their place. Have you successfully done what you're accusing the other guy of failing to do? Look at things from his point of view. You may see that you're the one who needs to make changes.

10. End confrontation with encouragement. Always give confrontation the "sandwich treatment." Sandwich the criticism between praise at the beginning and encouragement at the end. To leave a discouraged person without hope is cruel and vindictive. Goethe, the German poet said, "Correction does much, but encouragement does more. Encouragement after censure is as the sun after a shower."

In my effort to simplify things as much as possible, I have come up with one-word descriptions of the various ways people will respond to confrontation:

BYE. The "bye" people never profit from confrontation; they don't hang around long enough. Their egos are too fragile.

SPY. Spies become suspicious of everyone. They begin an investigation to find out who in the organization is out to get them. Often they will avoid risking a failure again.

FRY. Some people will simply get mad and either fly off at the handle or do a slow burn.

LIE. The liar has an excuse for every mistake. Therefore he never faces up to the reality of his situation.

CRY. Cry babies are overly sensitive and become hurt by confrontation. Unlike the "bye" people, criers hang around in hopes that people will see how mistreated they are and sympathize with them. They have a martyr complex.

SIGH. These people have a "That's-too-bad,-but-there's-nothing-I-can-do-about-it" attitude. They don't accept any responsibility for making right the wrong.

FLY. This category of people takes criticism and flies with it. They learn from it and become better because of it.

Which category has fit you in the past? Are there changes you need to make before you can take criticism and fly with it? I challenge you to start today

PUT IT TO WORK

People Principles

☐ If you're willing to stand apart from the crowd, you're putting yourself in a vulnerable position. Count on some degree of criticism.

☐ When you are willing to stick your neck out, someone will want to chop it off. Don't let that threat keep you from being all you can be. Rise above it.

☐ The question is not "Will I be confronted with criticism?" but "How can I handle and learn from criticism and confrontation?"

☐ If you develop the ability to laugh at yourself, you will be much more relaxed when given or giving criticism.

☐ A negative attitude toward criticism can be more destructive than the criticism itself. A chip on the shoulder indicates wood higher up.

☐ In order to build strong relationships we need to know how to take criticism gracefully, but there are also times when we will have to be the critic. It is possible to confront without ruining a relationship.

Putting the Principles to Work:
I will apply the principles from this chapter to my relationships with people in the following ways:

1.

2.

3.

Further Study:
Your Attitude: Key to Success, John C. Maxwell
Helping Those Who Don't Want Help, Marshall Shelley

10.

BEING A PERSON PEOPLE TRUST

Building integrity into your relationships

Trust is crucial in any type of relationship, whether it be within a family, a business, a church congregation, or in a friendship. When this important foundation exists, strong, positive relationships are built and fed by encouragement and consistency. People who receive a high level of trust have developed their character and have earned the right to be trusted.

Twenty-five years ago I read a book by W. Curry Mavis, *Advancing the Smaller Church*, in which he said something that I still buy today. He said the greatest problem in most local churches is low morale. If you can get the people's spirits lifted, then things can happen. High morale is the result of the leader's confidence and trust in the people he leads. Morale is conveyed through a sense of common purpose and it produces a state of psychological and emotional well-being based on such factors as principle, conduct, confidence, and teaching.

Trust depends very little upon a person's name, his station in life, how much money he has in the bank, or his position. The key to consistent and dependable trust lies in the *character* of the person who leads. Whether we lead in our homes, businesses, or churches we are responsible for being trustworthy. We have to prove by example that we are as good as our word. There is absolutely no other way to establish a reputation for being trustworthy except to be trustable.

Charlie Brown has an incredible trust in human nature. Every once in a while cartoonist Charles Schultz shows us Lucy holding a football for Charlie Brown to kick. With an assuring smile on her face, Lucy insists that she can be trusted; she vows that she will not cause him the pain and humiliation of falling on his backside by removing the ball just before he kicks. Charlie Brown always takes a running charge at the ball and Lucy always pulls back the football, causing him to kick at the air and hit the ground. But he continues to make the attempt, confident that one day Lucy will demonstrate trustworthiness.

Most of us are not as naive as Charlie Brown. Before we are willing to put our trust in someone, we want to see that they are reliable. We're not willing to give too many second chances where lack of trust is a factor.

You can help develop trust in people by applying the key principles which follow.

Demonstrate What You Want to Instill

People need to see what they ought to be. A cartoon punch line read, "No matter what you teach the child, he insists on behaving like his parents." That's certainly a humbling truth for all parents.

Dennis the Menace often reinforces this truth. On one occasion, while holding the remnants of a tricycle which has been smashed to smithereens, Dennis the Menace asked his dad, "What are some of those words you say when you hit a bad golf shot?" He had learned that there was a certain way to behave when you're frustrated.

When I disciple others it is important to me to *be* what I teach or ask others to do. This is a crucial truth: We teach what we *know*, but we reproduce what we *are*. To teach others to do right is wonderful. To do right is even more wonderful! It may be a harder way to teach, but it's a much easier way to learn.

Dr. James Dobson, psychologist and author, tells us that kids begin to buy in to your spiritual guidance and direction in the area of values at about five years of age! During the early years of your child's life you are the primary role model, the most significant person in his or her life. If what you say is different from what you do, your child will choose to imitate what you do every time. In the words of Zig Ziglar, "Your children pay more attention to what you do than what you say." So the most valuable gift you can give your little ones is the example of a clear, consistent, disciplined approach to faith in God. It is most important that they see this beginning in their earliest years. What they learn and establish in their lives during these years can go a long way in getting them through the tumult of adolescence.

Encouragement Causes Growth

Encouragement has the effect of a gentle rain; it causes steady growth. The secret of Andrew Carnegie's genius for developing others was his ability to encourage good qualities, while holding faultfinding to a minimum. Confidence withers under faultfinding, as the following story about a singer illustrates.

She made her debut at the age of five in a church cantata. The choir director told her parents that someday she would be a great singer. The entire congregation had fallen in love with the little girl in pigtails—her voice, her poise, her instinctive stage presence.

She continued to sing and after college went to study music in Chicago. One of her instructors was a man named Fritz. Though he was old enough to be her father she fell in love with him and they were married. Wherever she sang Fritz would be there. Afterward he would point out all of her mistakes, constantly urging her toward perfection. In their apartment he set alarm clocks telling her it was time for practice. His trained ear caught the slightest imperfection.

Gradually her singing got worse instead of better. Musical directors stopped hiring her. Under the constant barrage of criticism, her spirit was breaking, she was losing her assurance, her naturalness.

While her career was plummeting, the husband died. Even after he was gone, she sang little, haunted by his familiar voice pointing out her errors. A couple of years later she happened to meet a jolly, carefree salesman named Roger. He knew little about music, but liked her voice and encouraged her to take up singing again. In a few months they were married.

Friends noticed that she seemed to be regaining her self-assurance, and that the strident quality had left her voice. It was pure and joyous, as it had been when she was a child. Now musical directors eagerly sought her out.

The woman's first husband, though well-intentioned, had broken both her spirit and her voice by constant faultfinding. The second man, by contrast, gave her the encouragement she needed by stressing only the good in her.

I have yet to find the person, whatever his or her station in life, who did not perform better under a spirit of approval than under criticism. There are enough critics in the world; what we need are more cheerleaders!

You can learn to be an encourager by practicing the following procedures.

1. Appreciate people for who they are. This truth is dramatically played out in the lives of children. They have a way of mirroring what they hear about themselves. Recently I watched a talk show which was devoted to the subject of teenage suicide. More and more teenagers are attempting suicide as an escape from the demands of life. They feel they can never measure up to the standards of performance expected by parents and others. They feel appreciated only when they've done well, not because they're unique and priceless individuals. As a result, many kids see life as a no-win situation.

2. Anticipate they will do their best. When working with people I always try to look at them not as they are, but as what they can be. By anticipating that the vision will become real, it's easy for me to encourage them as they stretch. Raise your anticipation level and you raise their achievement level.

3. Admire their accomplishments. Thank them and praise them for what they have done. Remember, man does not live by bread alone; sometimes he needs a little buttering up. Remember the effect of praise on the singer.

4. Accept your personal responsibility. If you oversee people you are responsible to take the heat at times. I developed a tremendous admiration for Coach Bear Bryant when I heard him say:

> I'm just a plowhand from Arkansas, but I have learned how to hold a team together—how to lift some men up, how to calm down others, until finally they've got one heartbeat together, a team. There's just three things I'd ever say: If anything goes bad, I did it. If anything goes semi-good, then we did it. If anything goes real good, then you did it. That's all it takes to get people to win football games for you.

Again, let me emphasize the importance of character in developing trust. Bishop Able Muzore tells of a critical period in his life when he had been asked by his people to lead the African National Council. He knew that all previous leaders in Rhodesia who had been critical of unjust government policies toward Black Rhodesians had been either deported from the country, put in a restricted camp, or killed.

He struggled with his decision and prayed as he had never prayed before. He did not want to be killed, or deported, or placed in a restricted camp, yet his people were calling him to lead them. During the time he was struggling with his decision, a friend handed him this poem:

> People are unreasonable, illogical, and self-centered—love them anyway!

If you do good, people will accuse you of selfish
ulterior motives—do good anyway!

If you are successful you will win false friends and
true enemies—succeed anyway!

The good you do today will be forgotten tomorrow—do good anyway!

Honesty and frankness make you vulnerable—be
honest and frank anyway!

The biggest people with the biggest ideas can be
shot down by the smallest people with the smallest minds—think big anyway!

People favor underdogs but follow only top dogs—
fight for some underdog anyway!

What you spend years building may be destroyed
overnight—build anyway!

Give the world the best you've got and you'll get
kicked in the teeth—give the world the best
you've got anyway!

Believe the Best

Develop a person's expectation level by believing the best
in him or her. When you look up to people they begin to
look up to their dreams. A few weeks ago I spoke to some
salespeople about their expectation level of those they
oversee. I explained that how we view a person is reflected
by how we treat a person. If we have a high expectation
level and believe in people, we will encourage them. Again,
it is the principle of seeing people not as they are but as
they can be.

The business manager at our church placed his house on
the market. One Saturday he and his wife posted signs all
over the neighborhood announcing an open house. As they
prepared for the day, Ken told his wife Mary Lynn, "We're
going to have all kinds of people come in and out of the
house today, most with absolutely no resources or inten-
tion of buying. But we're going to treat them all the same—
as if they were our guests."

Sure enough they had dozens of people come through

just to look. One young couple in their early twenties asked to see the house. They announced that they were newly married, she had no job, and he was just starting a new job. After the tour they extended their thanks and left. Ken and Mary Lynn announced to each other, "Well, we'll never see them again." But in just thirty minutes they saw a very expensive car drive up and park in front of the house. The same young couple returned—this time with mom and dad. The father shook Ken's hand and said, "The kids sure liked your home. This will be a cash sale; how short can we make the escrow?"

I'm certain that Ken and Mary Lynn's high level of anticipation filtered through to each person who crossed the threshold of their home. They had no idea what benefits that positive attitude would bring.

Many people, unfortunately, have a low personal expectation level. We need to know how to develop a dream for others and then share it with them. Begin by seeing it for them. We can all learn a lesson from the "four-eyed fish." These odd-looking creatures are native to the equatorial waters of the western Atlantic region. The technical name of this genus of fish is anableps, meaning "those that look upward," because of their unusual eye structure. Unique among vertebrates, the anableps have two-tiered eyes, with the upper and lower halves of each eyeball operating independently and having separate cornea and irises. The upper eyes protrude above the surface of the water and enable the anableps to search for food and to spot enemies in the air. The lower eyes remain focused in the water, functioning in the usual fishlike fashion. Thus, in rather ordinary ways these four-eyed fish navigate with ease in the waters of their environment. But, in addition, the anableps enjoy a remarkable capacity to sustain life by participating in the "higher" world above their primary environment. They see in both worlds.

If we can develop four eyes, two for seeing what is and two for seeing what might be, we can help others dream. Everyone needs to be exposed to a vision. Unfortunately, not everyone will go for it. Pursue it with those who are ready to stretch.

Help Others Be Successful

Develop confidence in others by helping them experience success. We've all heard the slogan, "It doesn't matter whether you win or lose"—until you lose! Winning increases our self-image, our outlook on life, and lifts our expectation level. It gives us the confidence that we can succeed again. How can you help make another person successful? It's fairly simple. Make sure their gifts and abilities match their tasks. Otherwise you set them up for sure failure. Discern their gifts and desires and match them to the opportunities available. When you have the ability to suit them to a job at which they can succeed, an incredible bond of trust and respect develops.

Everyone enjoys the glory of the spotlight and the opportunity to shine. But it's a sign of a mature person who will afford another that prized position of recognition. For example, I have shared my faith in Christ effectively for many years but I also train others to develop their witnessing skills. If I sense a prospect is extremely open and receptive to making a commitment to Christ, I allow the trainee the opportunity of leading the person to Christ. Likewise, if the trainee is struggling, I will jump in to assist. Success for the leader is a single victory. However, when the protege experiences success, it becomes a double win.

Equip People for Future Growth

"Give a man a fish and he eats for a day. Teach a man to fish and he eats for a lifetime." In other words, if you want to help him, don't give him a fish, give him a fishing rod. This principle applies to personal growth. You and I can't grow another person, but we can give him the equipment to develop himself. We do this by first showing him that the growth is beneficial; we whet his appetite for growth. Then we expose him to people like himself who have moved out and become successful; we prove that it can be done. And finally, we provide an opportunity for him to use his new equipment. And we stand back and encourage.

In the late 1800's a salesman from the East arrived at a frontier town somewhere on the Great Plains. As he was talking with the owner of the general store, a rancher came in. The owner excused himself to take care of the customer. The salesman couldn't help overhearing the conversation. It seems the rancher wanted credit for the things he needed.

"Are you doing any fencing this spring, Josh?" asked the storekeeper.

"Sure am, Will," said the rancher.

"Fencing in or fencing out?"

"Fencing in. Taking in another 360 acres across the creek."

"Good to hear it, Josh. You got the credit. Just tell Harry out back what you need."

The salesman couldn't make much sense of this. "I've seen all kinds of credit systems," he said, "but never one like that. How does it work?"

"Well," said the storekeeper, "it's like this. If a man's fencing out, that means he's running scared with what he's got. But if he's fencing in, he's growing and getting bigger. He's got hope. I always give credit to a man who's fencing in!"

Give people the encouragement they need to fence in. Provide the encouragement and the know-how for them to expand their horizons. The rewards will not only come back to them, they will come back to you. By believing in people and helping them trust in themselves, you have established a relationship in which everyone involved is a winner.

PUT IT TO WORK

People Principles

☐ People who receive a high level of trust have developed their character and have earned the right to be trusted. When this important foundation exists, strong, positive relationships are built and are fed by encouragement and consistency.

☐ Trust depends very little on a person's name, his station in life, how much money he has in the bank, or his position. The key to consistent and dependable trust lies in the character of the person who leads.

☐ Keys to being a trustable person:
Demonstrate what you want to instill.
Be an encourager.
Believe the best in others.
Help others experience success.
Equip people for future growth.

Putting the Principles to Work:

I will apply the principles from this chapter to my relationships with people in the following ways:

1.

2.

3.

Further Study:

How to Have a Better Relationship with Anybody, James Hitt

How to Get Along with People in the Church, A. Donald Bell

11.

DEVELOPING A WINNING TEAM

Learning how to help others become successful

One night after working quite late, I grabbed a copy of *Sports Illustrated*, hoping its pages would lull me to sleep. It had the opposite effect, though. On the back cover of this issue was an advertisement that caught my eye and got my mental juices flowing. It featured a picture of John Wooden, the coach who led the U.C.L.A. Bruins for many years.

The caption said: "The guy who puts the ball through the hoop has ten hands." They called John Wooden the wizard of Westwood. In a span of twelve seasons he brought ten national basketball championships to U.C.L.A. Two back-to-back championships are almost unheard of in the competitive sports world, but he led the Bruins to seven titles in a row! It took a consistently high level of superior play; it took good coaching and hard practice. But the key to the Bruin's success was Coach Wooden's unyielding concept of teamwork.

This ad was exciting because it said so much about teamwork. When a basketball player becomes a high scorer, we make him a hero. But could he have done it had he been facing the opposition alone? I doubt it. It took eight other hands to prepare the way for his successful baskets. It was a team effort all the way.

In Genesis 11:1-6 we can read a biblical account of team effort: the building of the Tower of Babel. In this account we find some key concepts that can help you build an effective team.

> Now the whole earth used the *same language* and the *same words*. And it came about as they journeyed east, that they found a plain in the land of Shinar and settled there. And *they said to one another, "Come let us* make bricks and burn them thoroughly." And they used brick for stone, and they used tar for mortar. And *they said, "Come let us* build for ourselves a city, and a tower whose top will reach into heaven, and let us make for ourselves a name; lest we be scattered abroad over the face of the whole earth." And the Lord came down to see the city and the tower which the sons of men had built. And the Lord said, "Behold, *they are one people,* and *they all have the same language.* And this is what they began to do, and *now nothing which they purpose to do will be impossible for them.* (Italics added.)

I'll stop here long enough to point out that their efforts were for a wrong cause. But God saw here the incredible power of a group of people coming together. In verses one through six we see how to develop a successful team. There are only two essential ingredients: first, a common goal, and second, the ability to communicate that goal. "Come let us build for ourselves ... a tower" expresses both a desire to work together and a goal.

That phrase also expressed a motive—"for ourselves." God didn't like what he saw because it was for an evil purpose; therefore, in verse seven we read that He decides to stop the team. Nevertheless, this account provides an excellent example of the importance of good teamwork.

It's easy to understand a sports team. Their goal is clear because lights and numbers flash when they have reached it. You know they are a team because they wear identical uniforms. Their purpose and focus is clear because all eyes and attention are centered on the ball, and all motion swiftly moves toward it.

But there are other kinds of teams that are harder to analyze. Wearing the same uniform, whether it be a baseball cap or a clerical collar, working in the same office, or being paid by the same organization does not make a team. Uniformity is not the key to successful teamwork. The glue that holds a team together is unity of purpose.

I was taught something about teamwork early in high school when I played basketball. We had some talented guys, and all but two were big enough to stuff the ball in the basket. We were expected to be third or fourth in the state, but our team had a problem. There was a tremendous division between the juniors and seniors. On the starting lineup we had two juniors and three seniors and instead of throwing the ball to the most open man, we threw it to the fellow who was in our same grade. Our team was divided; we had fights in the locker room as well as on the court. Because of the lack of teamwork we did not achieve what we could have with all the talent represented on that team. Our goals were not shared.

Winning Teams Play to Win

There are four major attributes which characterize a winning team. First of all, a winning team plays to win. Team members realize that wins and losses are often determined by attitude alone. The difference between playing to win and playing not to lose is often the difference between success and mediocrity.

Remember when the Olympics were held in Los Angeles a few years ago? There was an interesting article about the best of the best who competed in those games. The bottom line was that the difference between a gold-medal-winner and a silver-medal-winner is not skill, it's attitude.

When I moved to the West Coast, the only thing I left my heart tied to was Ohio State football. I continued to follow the team and catch Ohio State games on television whenever possible. Their trips to the Rose Bowl were especially exciting for me. But anybody who knows anything about college football knows that when any of the Big Ten comes to the West Coast to play, it's usually a West Coast victory. Though the eastern teams often had superior talent, they often did not take a risk. I think the Big Ten teams play not to lose—not a winning strategy.

Winning Teams Take Risks

The second characteristic of winning teams is that they are risk-takers. My philosophy of life is to throw the ball and go for it! Don't move three yards and huddle together and hope. Take a risk and let what happens happen. It will make the difference between a successful team and a mediocre one. On my office wall hangs a plaque that says, "I don't have to survive." I want my team to perform above the level of mediocrity. It's far better to try and fail than to fail to try.

The following poem appeared in Ann Landers' column. Each line contains a truth and a test:

> To laugh is to risk appearing a fool.
> To weep is to risk appearing sentimental.
> To reach out for another is to risk involvement.
> To expose feelings is to risk rejection.
> To place your dreams before the crowd is to risk ridicule.
> To love is to risk not being loved in return
> To go forward in the face of overwhelming odds is to risk failure.
>
> But risks must be taken because the greatest hazard in life is to risk nothing.
> The person who risks nothing does nothing, has nothing, is nothing.
> He may avoid suffering and sorrow, but he cannot learn, feel, change, grow, or love.

Chained by his certitudes, he is a slave.
Only a person who takes risks is free.

I love the story about the old farmer, ragged and bare-footed, who sat on the steps of his tumbledown shack, chewing on a stem of grass. A passerby stopped and asked if he might have a drink of water. Wishing to be sociable, the stranger engaged the farmer in some conversation.

"How is your cotton crop this year?"

"Ain't got none," replied the farmer.

"Didn't you plant any cotton?" asked the passerby.

"Nope," said the farmer, " 'fraid of boll weevils."

"Well," asked the newcomer, "how's your corn doing?"

"Didn't plant none," replied the farmer, " 'fraid there wasn't going to be enough rain."

"Well," asked the inquisitive stranger, "what did you plant?"

"Nothing," said the farmer, "I just played it safe."

A lot of well-intentioned people live by the philosophy of this farmer, and never risk upsetting the apple cart. They would prefer to "play it safe." These people will never know the thrill of victory, because to win a victory one must risk a failure.

C.T. Studd made a great statement about risk-taking: "Are gamblers for gold so many and gamblers for God so few?" This is the same great missionary who, when cautioned against returning to Africa because of the possibility of his martyrdom, replied, "Praise God, I've just been looking for a chance to die for Jesus." How can a guy like that fail? He has everything to win and nothing to lose.

Winning Teams Keep Improving

The third characteristic of winning teams is they continue to try harder. They realize that when they're through improving, they're through. It's interesting to note that during the 1980's no team playing professional basketball, baseball, or football has won a World Series or national championship for two years in a row It's hard to stay on top.

Once you get there, you tend to try to maintain the situation and hang onto the glory. This is a big mistake, because there's always someone below who is hungry for victory. They'll make the necessary sacrifices and take the risks to get the top. It's easier to win when you've got nothing to lose. It never pays to rest on your laurels; you must be willing to give them up if you want to keep winning.

Lon Woodrum, a dear friend of mine in his late 80's, continues to be an outstanding speaker, writer, and poet. He has set a goal for himself to read a book a day. I questioned him about that, thinking that at his age he should be taking life a little easier. He said, "John, I have a tendency to get lazy. I want my 86-year-old mind to keep growing and learning. I want to die with a book in my hand." Lon is going to live until he dies. I know a lot of people who are breathing, but who are already dead!

Art Linkletter put it this way:

I never want to be
What I want to be,
Because there's always something out there
Yet for me.
I get a kick out of living
In the here and now,
But I never want to feel
I know the best way how.
There's always one hill higher,
With a better view,
Something waiting to be learned
That I never knew.
Till my days are over,
Never fully fill my cup;
Let me go on
Growing up.

The highest reward for man's improvement is not what he gets for it; it's what he becomes as a result of it. Ask yourself why you are trying to improve. Is it to receive something for it? If so, that's the wrong motive. Try to improve because it makes you a better person.

Winning Team Members Care about Each Other

The fourth characteristic of a winning team is that each member cares about the success of every other member. They enhance each other. Andrew Carnegie realized that before he could be successful, he needed to make his employees successful. He once said, "It marks a big step in your development when you realize that other people can help you do a better job than you could do alone." In the business world he was known for his outstanding development of people. Once he had thirty millionaires working for him. That's when a million dollars was a million dollars. Someone asked Carnegie how he induced that many millionaires to work for him. He replied that they weren't millionaires when he hired them; they made it while they were with him.

"How did you find such men?" people inquired.

Carnegie answered, "It's like mining for gold. When you start, you may have to move tons of dirt to find a gold nugget . . . but when you start mining for gold, you overlook the dirt."

Charles Brower said, "Few people are successful unless a lot of other people want them to be."

Do you recall when Edmond Hillary and his native guide, Tenzing, made their historic climb of Mt. Everest? Coming down from the peak Hillary suddenly lost his footing. Tenzing held the line taut and kept them both from falling by digging his ax into the ice. Later Tenzing refused any special credit for saving Hillary's life; he considered it a routine part of the job. As he put it; "Mountain climbers always help each other."

If you're an old enough sports fan, you'll remember the days of the Boston Celtics and Red Auerbach. When he knew they had won the game, he always lit up his cigar. That was his trademark. Whenever he lit his cigar he sent out smoke signals to the other team—it's our win! When I can tell that my team, the Skyline staff, is working together on a winning project, I mentally light a cigar!

Just how do we develop a winning team? Three key areas together determine the success of the team: hiring, firing, and inspiring. Let's consider each one in turn.

Hiring Right

The most important feature of any organization is the quality of the staff. Great athletic coaches know it takes more than inspiration to win; they must have talent. Therefore coaches take a major hand in the hiring. After all, staffs that just happen get happenstance results!

Most pastors of large churches tell me that staffing is their number-one frustration. A few years ago I was in a forum with pastors of some of the largest churches across the country. Our agenda included a variety of topics for discussion. The very first item was the question, "What things frustrate you the most in ministry?" It is no exaggeration to say that 80 percent of the next two and one half days were spent discussing staff and staff-related problems. Rather than moving with their staffs toward mutual goals, many of these senior pastors were preoccupied with staff-related problems.

Perhaps you may be reading this and feeling that because you have a smaller church with only one other staff member, this section is not relevant to your situation. Don't make the mistake of thinking you can get by with inferior staff members because you are small. The opposite is true. In a business of 100 employees, if one is inferior, the loss is only 1 percent. But if a church has a payroll of two, and one is inferior, the loss is 50 percent.

Kurt Einstein in *Success* magazine said that hiring the wrong person is an extremely costly mistake. If that employee is fired within six months, it costs the company at least two years salary. You can see the damaging financial effect of not hiring correctly.

There are three hindrances to hiring outstanding staff, especially in Christian circles. *The first is in getting ref-*

erences from previous employers. Honest references are almost always sabotaged by tolerance, because no one wants to blow the whistle on a poor worker. It is my Christian responsibility to be as objective as I can when giving a reference. To do otherwise would be deceitful. An employer does an employee no favors by recommending him for a job for which he is not suited.

Another hindrance to hiring top-quality staff is the fact that you are probably a small organization and *smaller organizations have less to offer than larger organizations.* But take my advice: Don't let the size of your church or organization determine the quality of your staff. Go for the winner and offer him or her your vision for the future. Don't offer your present situation unless you plan to camp there permanently. Hire a person who can grasp your dream. If they understand that you have the ability to make that dream a reality, they may be willing to leave a comfortable situation to move into an exciting one.

Rick Warren, pastor of the Saddleback Valley Community Church in Southern California, showed this type of entrepreneurial spirit when he responded to God's call to plant a church. As the assistant pastor of a church with more than 3,000 members he became the interim pastor when the senior pastor left. The congregation approached Rick with the possibility of taking the leadership of that church. He turned them down. Captured by his vision of planting a new church, he gave up what was in his hand.

The third hindrance in hiring outstanding staff is not knowing what qualities to look for in prospective staff members. Perhaps you know what job needs to be done but are not sure of the qualities a person needs to do the job best. Here's a hiring formula that will help you *RATE* an individual:

Relationship + **A**ttitude x **T**alent + **E**xpectation = **P**roduction

Let's consider the importance of each of these words.

Relationships

Kurt Einstein of *Success* magazine says of this important characteristic in a work-related situation: "87 percent of all people fail, not because of capability but because of personality." People usually don't fail because they can't do the job, but because they can't get along with their coworkers.

If you work only for yourself, you may not need too many relational skills. However, if you work with people, you must have (or seek to develop) the ability to interact positively with them. Can you talk to people easily? Do you listen to them? Do you have a sense of humor and the ability to laugh at yourself without being sensitive and defensive? Do you enjoy people and working with them? Are you warm and approachable?

The leader of any group must exemplify certain relational essentials. First, he must respect his staff. They will not only absorb his respect, they will reflect it back to him. He also needs to provide open and honest two-way communication of all issues. Open communication establishes an atmosphere of trust which is essential if a group of people is to function as a team.

Some leaders have a great deal of insecurity and are, therefore, fearful of trusting those with whom they work. This type of leader looks at others with a suspicious mind, dwelling on possible underlying motives: Is a staff member out to take over their position? Determine if your fears are real or not. If they are not, dispel them and trust your people.

A leader will be hurt in one of two ways. He can be nontrusting and hold his people at a distance, never sharing or being open with them. Though his feelings may not be hurt because he won't allow anyone to get close to him, he will be hurt in other ways because no one will ever help him. His will be a lonely trip with no one to hug, love, or share the joy of ministry. On the other hand a leader can choose to be open and transparent and chance the possibility of being hurt by one who takes advantage of that trust. That is a risk worth taking. I would hate to think of the rich, deep friendships I would never have developed had I not risked trusting people.

Attitudes
This is the tiebreaker for hiring a team member. If I have interviewed two people who are on equal footing, their attitudes will always determine my decision. It doesn't matter how capable a person is, if he has a negative mind-set, he will be destructive to the team. A negative mind-set manifests itself in a critical spirit and nonsupport of other team members. If I ever sense that this is a problem with a staff member, that person will soon be looking for a new job. I can help a person improve his abilities, but only he can change his attitude.

Talent
Businessman Jim Cafcart looks for three things in helping people become productive:

☐ *Talent.* What are they good at?

☐ *Interests.* What are they fascinated by?

☐ *Values.* What do they believe in?

Interests and values pretty much determine how and to what extent one uses his talents. It is a fact that we are not equal in dislikes. The Parable of the Talents in the Gospel of Matthew certainly underlines this truth. The ability of the employer to discern the gifts and abilities of potential employees is essential for the success of the team.

Expectations
A leader needs to know what his staff members expect of him and the staff needs to know what's expected of them. Here are some of my expectations of staff members:

☐ *Growth.* I expect continual personal growth and departmental growth. Each staff member should be stretching to his or her utmost and the results should be visible. As this happens, each area of leadership will feel the positive effect.

☐ *Teamwork.* The whole is more important than its parts. Though each member of the team should be producing results in his or her own department, this growth is subordinate to the health and growth of the body as a whole.

☐ *Leadership.* They must learn how to influence people and develop people. This generally happens as staff members stretch and grow themselves.

In *Leadership* magazine I once saw a cartoon of a pastor sitting at his desk talking on the telephone. The caption read, "Well then, will you take two secretaries and one choir director for one assistant pastor and a singles man?" This leads me to the next aspect of staffing, firing staff members.

Firing a Worker

Being released from one's responsibilities can have a devastating effect on a person. It is not an action to be taken on a whim but only after careful, prayerful consideration. The following questions can help in making the decision. First, *has the church outgrown the pastor or has the pastor outgrown the church?* It is not uncommon for either to happen. I know what it is like to realize that the challenge is gone and it is time to move on to other possibilities. I have also known churches to forge ahead while the pastor sat wringing his hands, wondering what to do with a situation beyond his control.

Before letting a staff member go, another question to ask is, *who believes this person needs to be replaced?* If I, as the pastor or leader, am the only one who believes a change needs to be made, then I should tread carefully. Perhaps there is a personality conflict that needs attention and resolution. When it's time for a change to be made, more than one person should be sensing that need. Other staff, members of the church board, other key associations, and even the staff member in question, will feel the need for this change. To guard against personal prejudices and unfair evaluations I yearly ask the church board to participate in an anonymous review of all the staff members. This provides a wide spectrum of the effectiveness of each staff member.

The third question to be answered: *What is the basis for the dismissal?* What grounds are serious enough to let someone go? By far the most important thing to review is moral integrity. When there is a basic character problem—lying, moral compromise, deceitfulness—a quick removal is in order. I am convinced that when a person has lost trust, his or her ministry and service is over within the Christian community. I certainly believe in forgiveness, rehabilitation, and restoration into fellowship, but not restoration to a position.

Other possible grounds for dismissal would include serious relational problems. If a person is chronically at odds with other members of the team, there is need for removal. Or when a staff member shows an obvious negative attitude toward the church or organization, it's time to let that person go. Negative thinking can spread like a cancer. Finally, if a staff member reveals a serious lack of ability that cannot be corrected, he or she should be released.

As the pastor, it is my responsibility to have the best person possible in each position. The church board holds me accountable for this. If I neglect to do this, then I am not keeping the church's highest potential as a priority. The board holds me accountable just as it does my staff. My own job is on the line if there is someone else who can better lead and serve.

If firing is necessary, just how do we make the transition a little smoother? Assume we have worked through the tough questions. We have tried to balance mercy with stewardship and forgiveness with accountability. The decision becomes clear; the person must be removed from ministry or work responsibility. Then what?

First of all, we do it personally. A letter or memo is too cruel and impersonal, allowing feelings of desertion to be magnified and bitterness to be cultivated. A personal encounter allows for tears, anger, and other emotions that accompany such a blow. It also gives opportunity for the person to raise questions. Obviously, the news should be delivered promptly and directly before some grapevine has a chance to reach the worker being terminated.

Do it gently. There is no need to write a twelve-page list of the person's shortcomings. In fact, that person should have had that twelve-page list several weeks prior and been given a probation period to work on his or her problems. When the dismissal is given the person may become angry or defensive and that is the time for a "soft answer." Gentleness, however, does not require dishonesty. If the person is ill-equipped for ministry or leadership, it is more harmful to pretend otherwise. Remember that *how* and *when* these messages are given can soften the blow.

Do it without bitterness or malice. Those who deliver the message of dismissal must be under the Holy Spirit's control. Emotional outbursts or attacks on the person's character are counterproductive to the goal of the person's growth and eventual healing.

Close off responsibilities quickly. The longer a lame duck has to drag on in the job, the lower his or her productivity and the more he depresses the zeal of others. A drawn-out firing process opens the door to lobbying for a reversal and excuses for poor performance. Also, it is possible for the leader to lose his objectivity when he starts getting pressure from pocket groups. He will then begin second-guessing his decision to fire.

Be discriminating. "All the facts" do not need to be divulged to those whose interest is to slander or gossip. The details of a moral failure may serve to titillate warped appetites for scandal more than to promote healing in the body of Christ. Choose your words cautiously. Do not make matters worse than they are and needlessly jeopardize the person's future.

Anticipate the person's reactions and be prepared with your answers. Also consider the effect on those who are close to the person. How might you help those who may be hurt or offended in this change. Do you need to be involved in some emotional healing? Finally, consider where that person might go if possible, and try to help them in that transition.

Inspiring Your People

Harold S. Geneen, former Director, President and CEO of IT and T said, "The essence of leadership is the ability to inspire others to work together as a team—to stretch for a common objective."

The leader needs to pave the way for those following by exemplifying a positive, hopeful attitude. A leader motivates his team toward the end result by continually reminding team members of the overall vision and the importance of accomplishing the goal. When the leader communicates clear expectations, he also gives his people a freedom to create. Most importantly, a leader expresses the most profound inspiration when he believes in his people—when they feel and know that he thinks they are the best and his total confidence is in them.

E.E. Kenyon of American Weekly shared this story of a surefire way to inspire the team (though not one I would recommend). The normally sourfaced boss smiled genially at the salesmen he had called together for a meeting. "Well, gentlemen," he said, "I've called you in to announce a big sales contest which I am starting immediately and which I will personally supervise."

There was an excited murmur from the assembled salesmen, and an eager voice from the rear called out: "What does the winner get, Mr. Smithson?"

"He gets," announced the boss, "to keep his job."

PUT IT TO WORK

People Principles
☐ Uniformity is not the key to successful teamwork. The glue that holds a team together is unity of purpose.
☐ Characteristics of winning teams:

They play to win.
They take risks.
They keep improving.
They care about each other.

☐ People who prefer to "play it safe" will never know the thrill of victory. To win a victory, one must risk failure.

☐ The highest reward for man's improvement is not what he gets for it, it's what he becomes as a result of it.

☐ It marks a big step in your development when you realize that other people can help you do a better job than you could do alone.

☐ Relationships + Attitude x Talent + Expectation = Production

☐ The essence of leadership is the ability to inspire others to work together as a team—to stretch for a common objective.

Putting the Principles to Work:
I will apply the principles from this chapter to my relationships with people in the following ways:

1.

2.

3.

Further Study:
People Power, John R. Noe
You and Your Network, Fred Smith